MAKING MATH
MEANINGFUL

A Student's Workbook
for Mathematics
in Class 7

Jamie York

 Floris
Books

Contents

To the Student (and Parent)

Class Seven is perhaps the most important year academically. In maths, Class 7 is when 'real maths' begins; up until now, you have been learning mostly just arithmetic. Some of the key themes for this year are measurement, ratios, percentages, the Pythagorean Theorem and algebra. All of this will be needed for studying maths in Class 8, and especially in the Upper School. Remember that struggling can be an important part of learning math. Often, students enter Class 7 feeling weak in maths, but with hard work and perseverance, they leave Class 7 strong in maths and ready to study many interesting and challenging topics in the coming years.

Some tips for using this workbook

- Make sure your work is readable and easy to follow.
- If there isn't enough room on the worksheet, then *show your work on a separate sheet,* making sure you write down the worksheet number and problem number, so you can easily find it later.
- If you get stuck on one problem, then go on to another problem, and come back later to the one that you were stuck on.
- While working on a problem from one worksheet, it may be helpful to refer back to a problem that you did on a previous worksheet.
- **Fractions.** All answers to fraction problems should be reduced. Don't give answers as improper fractions, but, instead, convert them to mixed numbers (for example, leave your final answer as 3¼ instead of ¹³⁄₄).
- **Division**. Answers for division problems

may be rounded to three significant digits, unless the problem states you should leave your answer as an exact decimal, in which case you must continue until it repeats or ends. For example, $2579 \div 56$ has an exact answer of $46.05\overline{357142857142}8$. Rounding it to three significant digits means that we go only as far as the fourth digit (which in this case is the second place after the decimal point, and is a 5), and then round up the previous digit for an answer of 46.1.

- **Answers involving time.** Answers requiring a measure of time should be given in separated units. Examples of this are: 1 day 6 hours instead of 1.25 days, and 3 hours 12 minutes instead of 3.2 hours.
- **Maths tricks.** A list of the maths tricks can be found at the back of this workbook.
- *Try your best on every problem.* Struggling and overcoming frustration are part of the process of doing maths. Even if you don't get a problem correct, you will learn by trying it, and then later seeing a correct solution.
- *Learn from your mistakes!* When you get a problem wrong, make sure you follow up on it; find your mistake, and learn how to do the problem correctly.

Getting help

The problems in this workbook are based upon the material found in our book, *A Teacher's Source Book for Mathematics in Classes 6–8.* The book has helpful explanations and examples, and is useful for parents (or tutors) who are helping their children with the worksheets found in this workbook.

Arithmetic – Sheet 1

Do it in your head

1) 400×3000

2) $8.46 \div 100$

3) 8.46×1000

4) 49×11

5) $42,000 \div 600$

6) 3.5×4

7) 105×108

8) $512 - 497$

9) 3×999

10) 24×99

11) 3.6×5

12) $3.6 \div 5$

13) $27 - 3.7$

14) 0.3×0.008

15) $0.4 \div 0.008$

16) 13^2

17) 25×6

18) 3^4

19) 5^3

20) What is half of $\frac{8}{13}$?

21) What is half of $\frac{7}{13}$?

Quickly estimate

22) $485,036 + 225,672$

23) 73364×587

24) $55,963 - 42,027$

25) $5273 \div 886$

Division

Leave your answers as exact decimals (perhaps repeating). Use short division for single digit divisors.

26) $25,286 \div 47$

27) $4277 \div 25$

28) $0.0073 \div 0.06$

29) $7809 \div 1.37$

34) $\frac{48}{49} \times \frac{35}{48}$

35) $5\frac{3}{5} \times 1\frac{3}{7}$

Fractions and decimals

30) Convert fractions to decimals and decimals to fractions.

36) $5\frac{3}{5} - 1\frac{3}{7}$

a) $^{93}/_{100}$

b) $^{9}/_{1000}$

c) $^{3}/_{5}$

d) $^{5}/_{6}$

37) $5\frac{3}{5} \div 1\frac{3}{7}$

e) $^{8}/_{11}$

f) $^{7}/_{24}$

g) 0.07

38) $\dfrac{5\frac{3}{5}}{1\frac{3}{7}}$

h) 0.043

i) 0.55

39) $(2\frac{1}{3})^2$

j) $0.\overline{3}$

k) 0.875

31) Convert to a mixed number: $\frac{45}{7}$

40) $48.3 + 1.24$

32) Convert to an improper fraction: $6\frac{4}{9}$

41) $48.3 - 1.24$

33) $\frac{5}{6} + \frac{2}{5}$

42) 48.3×1.24

Powers & roots

43) $(8)^2$

44) $(800)^2$

45) $(0.8)^2$

46) $(0.008)^2$

47) $(12)^3$

48) $(0.1)^5$

49) $\sqrt{64}$

50) $\sqrt{9,000,000}$

Arithmetic – Sheet 2

Do it in your head

1) 5.723×100

2) $435.7 \div 100$

3) 2.6×11

4) $0.14 \div 4$

5) $21 \div 33$

6) 15^2

7) 25×5

8) 25^2

9) 4^3

10) 5^4

11) 700×80

12) $160,000 \div 800$

13) What is $\frac{9}{20}$ doubled?

14) What is $\frac{9}{19}$ doubled?

15) 8.5×4

16) 1110×1080

17) $6023 - 5996$

18) 9999×4

19) 999×14

20) 6400×5

Divisibility
State whether each number is evenly divisible by anything from 2 to 12 (but not 7).

21) $1,033,857$

22) $1,378,416$

Division
Leave your answers as mixed numbers. Use short division for single digit divisors.

23) $1,033,857 \div 11$

24) $197,400 \div 389$

25) $1,378,416 \div 9$

Powers and roots

26) $(600)^2$

27) $(5.42)^2$

28) $(10)^5$

29) $(1)^{31}$

30) $(0.052)^3$

31) $\left(\frac{3}{4}\right)^2$

32) $\left(\frac{3}{4}\right)^3$

33) $\sqrt{4900}$

34) $\sqrt{1,000,000}$

35) $\sqrt[3]{1,000,000}$

36) $\sqrt[6]{1,000,000}$

Fractions and decimals

37) Convert to a fraction:

 a) 0.003

 b) 0.08

 c) 0.0125

 d) $0.\overline{5}$

 e) $0.\overline{6}$

38) Convert to a decimal:

 a) $\frac{4}{5}$

 b) $\frac{2}{11}$

 c) $\frac{3}{20}$

 d) $\frac{13}{99}$

 e) $\frac{11}{25}$

 f) $\frac{19}{60}$

39) Convert to a mixed number: $\frac{67}{12}$

40) Convert to an improper fraction:
$10\frac{3}{7}$

41) Reduce:

a) $\frac{210}{490}$

b) $\frac{12,600}{27,000}$

c) $\frac{27,000}{43,875}$

42) $\frac{5}{6} - \frac{1}{4}$

43) $\frac{5}{9} + \frac{21}{25}$

44) $\frac{5}{9} \times \frac{21}{25}$

45) $78\frac{2}{3} - 76\frac{3}{4}$

46) $\frac{3\frac{3}{4}}{5}$

47) $33 \div 3\frac{2}{3}$

Quickly estimate

48) 693×79

49) $2317 - 1824$

50) $51,893 + 16,256$

51) $36,478 \div 491$

Arithmetic – Sheet 3

Do it in your head

1) 0.043×100

2) $7649 \div 100$

3) $6400 \div 5$

4) 109^2

5) $5024 - 4986$

6) 6×9999

7) 15×2

8) 16×4

9) 15×3

10) 160×300

11) 18^2

12) 4^4

13) 0.03×0.4

14) 2^{10}

15) 120×90

16) 0.87×11

17) 25×3

18) $6.4 \div 4$

19) $220 \div 330$

20) 3^3

21) 4^5

22) $\sqrt{0.0049}$

Divisibility

23) State whether each number is evenly divisible by anything from 2 to 12 (but not 7):

  a) 156,750

  b) 18,698,988

24) Give the prime factorisation:
  a) 888

  b) 156,750

Division
Leave your answers as exact decimals (perhaps repeating).

25) $7.43 \div 6600$

26) $7 \div 0.303$

Powers and roots

27) $\sqrt{250,000}$

28) $\sqrt[3]{8}$

29) $\sqrt[4]{625}$

30) $\sqrt{64}$

31) $\sqrt[3]{64}$

32) $\sqrt[6]{64}$

33) $\sqrt[5]{32}$

34) $\sqrt[4]{16}$

35) $\sqrt[10]{1024}$

36) $\sqrt[4]{81}$

37) $\sqrt{810,000}$

38) $\sqrt[4]{810,000}$

39) $\sqrt{25,600,000,000}$

40) $\sqrt[4]{25,600,000,000}$

41) $(1.8)^2$

42) $(3\frac{1}{3})^3$

Fractions and decimals

43) Convert to a fraction:

a) 0.0041

b) 0.8

c) $0.\overline{5}$

d) 0.175

44) Convert to a decimal:

a) $\frac{5}{8}$

b) $\frac{1}{6}$

c) $\frac{1}{30}$

d) $\frac{33}{40}$

45) Convert to both a mixed number and an exact decimal

$\frac{5303}{18}$

46) 3.8×0.0045

47) $935.54 - 79.378$

48) $6\frac{2}{5} - 1\frac{3}{5}$

49) $6\frac{2}{5} \times 1\frac{3}{5}$

50) $6\frac{2}{5} \div 1\frac{3}{5}$

51) $12 \div 5\frac{1}{4}$

52) Quickly estimate:
a) 5249×48

b) $78,804 - 67,914$

c) $4083 \div 68$

d) 315×770

Arithmetic – Sheet 4

Do it in your head
1) $6.39 \div 1000$

2) 7.307×100

3) 9000^2

4) 13×4

5) 25×4

6) 16×3

7) 15×4

8) 3^4

9) 2^6

10) 5^3

11) $18,000 \div 2,000$

12) $(10.3)^2$

13) $350 \div 560$

14) $235,000 \times 4$

15) $8043 - 2987$

16) $8 \times 99,999$

17) 15×999

18) 6200×5

19) $740 \div 5$

20) $45 \div 54$

21) $21 - 3.1$

22) $0.03 \div 0.0006$

Divisibility
23) State whether each number is evenly divisible by anything from 2 to 12 (but not 7):
a) 40,832

b) 1,062,882

24) Give the prime factorisation:
a) 270,000

b) 1,062,882

Division

Leave your answers as mixed numbers.
Use short division for single digit divisors.

25) $45,277 \div 6$

26) $374,000 \div 42$

27) $387,031 \div 5,823$

Powers and roots

28) $\sqrt[3]{27}$

29) $\sqrt[5]{32}$

30) $\sqrt[3]{125}$

31) $\sqrt[5]{1024}$

32) $\sqrt[3]{1,000,000,000}$

33) $\sqrt[3]{8,000,000}$

34) $\sqrt{64,000,000}$

35) $\sqrt[6]{64,000,000}$

36) $(400)^3$

37) $(100)^4$

38) $(2\frac{4}{5})^2$

39) $(\frac{1}{3})^4$

40) $(\frac{2}{5})^4$

41) $(0.05)^4$

42) $(3.8)^3$

Fractions and decimals

43) Reduce each fraction:

a) $\dfrac{4800}{132,000}$

b) $\dfrac{350}{800}$

44) Convert to a fraction:
a) 0.75

b) 0.075

c) 0.875

d) 0.0875

e) 0.52

45) Convert to a decimal:

a) $\dfrac{7}{20}$

b) $\dfrac{4}{11}$

c) $\dfrac{73}{99}$

d) $\dfrac{13}{250}$

e) $\dfrac{61}{80}$

46) $53\frac{2}{7} - 49\frac{3}{4}$

47) $6\frac{2}{3} \div 5$

48) $\dfrac{3\frac{1}{5} - 1\frac{1}{2}}{\frac{3}{3/4}}$

Measurement – Sheet 1

The metric prefixes

c centi means $\frac{1}{100}$ of
m milli means $\frac{1}{1000}$ of
k kilo means 1000 of

The metric stairs

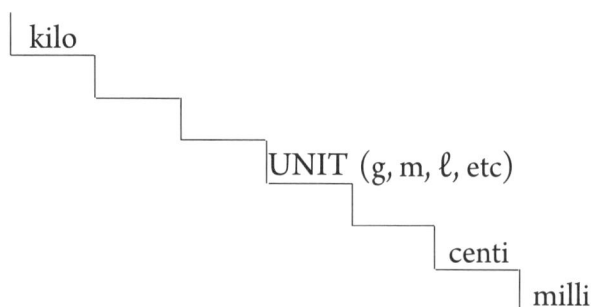

```
kilo
     UNIT (g, m, ℓ, etc)
              centi
                  milli
```

1 tonne = 1000 kg

Common imperial measures

Length

1 in	≈ 2.54 cm
1 ft = 12 in	≈ 30.5 cm
1 yd = 3 ft = 36 in	≈ 91.4 cm
1 mi = 1,760 yd = 5,280 ft	≈ 1.61 km

Weight

1 oz	≈ 28.4 g
1 lb = 16 oz	≈ 454 g
1 st = 14 lb	≈ 6.35 kg

Volume

1 fl oz	≈ 30 mℓ
1 pt = 20 fl oz	≈ 590 mℓ
1 gal = 8 pt	≈ 4.55 ℓ

Metric to imperial conversion

1 cm	≈ 0.39 in
1 m	≈ 39 in
(1 g	≈ 0.035 oz.)
1 kg	≈ 2.2 lb
1 ℓ	≈ 1.76 pt

1) State what each abbreviation stands for and state if it is length, weight or volume:

a) m

b) km

c) in

d) mi

e) mℓ

f) kg

g) st

h) lb

i) mg

2) Complete (round to three significant figures):

a) 2 pt = _____ fl oz

b) 2 pt ≈ _____ ℓ

c) 80 lb = _____ st _____ lb

d) 240 yd ≈ _____ m

e) 18 in ≈ _____ cm

f) 20 mi ≈ _____ km

g) 20 km ≈ _____ mi

h) 2.5 hr = _____ min

3) For each of the following, write a sign ($>$, $<$, $=$) between the two measurements to indicate which is bigger, or if they are equal:

a) 2 km   2 mi

b) 5 ℓ   5000 mℓ

c) 7 kg   700 g

d) 1 g   1 oz

e) 1 m   3 ft

f) 16 oz   1 lb

g) 300 yd   3 km

h) 3 cm   30 mm

i) 3050 mℓ   3 ℓ

j) 1 kg   2 lb

k) 1 in   1 cm

4) Circle the measurement that makes the most sense:

a) Weight of a typical person
200 kg   75 kg

b) Length of a car
7.5 ft   4.5 m

c) Diameter of an orange
75 mm   0.5 in

d) Volume of a glass
500 mℓ   2.7 ℓ

e) Length of a table
50 mm   1.5 m

Mental arithmetic

5) $71 \times 69 =$

6) $14 \times 16 =$

7) $59 \times 61 =$

8) $104 \times 108 =$

9) $2034 - 1988 =$

10) $2400 \div 800 =$

11) $84 \times 11 =$

12) $0.43 \times 10 =$

Review

13) State whether this number is evenly divisible by anything from 2 to 12 (but not 7): 3,405,888

14) Convert to a fraction.

a) $0.\overline{6}$

b) $0.\overline{8}$

c) 0.009

d) 0.3125

15) *Division.* Leave your answer as an exact decimal (perhaps repeating).

a) $0.0031 \div 0.55$

b) $724.8 \div 0.054$

16) $\sqrt{160{,}000}$

17) $\sqrt[4]{160{,}000}$

18) $(0.034)^2$

19) $230 - 0.23$

20) $\frac{10}{13} \times \frac{3}{13}$

21) $\frac{10}{13} \div \frac{3}{13}$

22) $\frac{10}{13} + \frac{3}{13}$

23) $\frac{10}{13} \times 1\frac{3}{10}$

24) $\frac{10}{13} + 1\frac{3}{10}$

Measurement – Sheet 2

1) Circle the measurement that makes the most sense:

a) Height of a chair
   0.75 m   2 m

b) Volume of a bathtub
   8 ℓ   500 ℓ

c) Weight of a full backpack
   5 kg   75 g

d) Thickness of a book
   0.5 m   14 mm

e) Distance that a ball is thrown
   0.015 km   470 m

Estimate

2) For each of the following, give an estimate (without measuring) using metric units.

a) Length of a tennis court

b) Weight of a piece of paper

c) Volume of a mouthful of water

d) Weight of a tennis ball

e) Volume of a tennis ball

f) Width of this paper

Add or subtract

3) Give answer in the smallest unit:

a) $8\,\ell - 348\,m\ell$

b) $5.3\,g + 570\,mg$

c) $3\,m + 53\,cm - 28\,mm$

d) $25\,ft - 7\,yd$

e) $\frac{1}{2}\,kg - 23\,g - 250\,mg$

f) $3\,hr - 90\,min$

4) Megan starts with a piece of wood that is 2 m long. She cuts off two pieces that are each 56 cm long, how long is the piece of wood that is left over (in metres)? (Ignore the width of the saw's blade.)

5) A group of 24 people have found 7.2 kg of gold. Assuming the gold is split evenly, how much gold does each person get (in grams)?

6) John's bottle holds 130 mℓ. How many trips will he have to make to completely fill up a 15 ℓ tub?

7) Mike ran 25 m in 15 seconds. Is this fast or slow?

8) A family is taking a 300 km road trip. How far have they travelled when they are ⅗ of the way there?

9) Complete:
a) 180 hr = _____ days

b) 7.32 g = _____ kg

c) 6.4 km = _____ m

d) 60 fl oz = _____ pt

e) 12 cm = _____ m

f) 3760 mm = _____ m

g) 3760 m = _____ km

h) 51 cm = _____ mm

i) 25.06 kg = _____ g

j) 65.75 ℓ = _____ mℓ

k) 3¾ tonne = _____ kg

l) 30 m = _____ km

Mental arithmetic

10) $41 \times 39 =$

11) $24 \times 26 =$

12) $89 \times 91 =$

13) $7 \div 999 =$

14) $480 \times 5 =$

15) $55 \times 4 =$

16) $212 - 198 =$

17) $6000 \div 9000 =$

Review

18) *Short Division.* Leave your answer as a mixed number:
a) $76{,}234 \div 5$

b) $400{,}000 \div 7$

19) $\sqrt{64}$

20) $\sqrt[3]{64}$

21) $\sqrt[6]{64}$

22) $\sqrt[3]{64{,}000{,}000}$

23) Convert to a decimal:
a) $\dfrac{19}{20}$

b) $\dfrac{10}{11}$

c) $\dfrac{79}{99}$

24) Reduce:
a) $\dfrac{40}{64}$

b) $\dfrac{312}{744}$

25) $53\frac{1}{3} - 49\frac{2}{3}$

26) 87.6×0.069

27) *Challenge*

$$\frac{\frac{5\frac{1}{3}}{2/3}}{\frac{4}{5} + \frac{3 - \frac{1}{5}}{4}}$$

Measurement – Sheet 3

Add or subtract

1) Give answer in the largest unit:

a) 3 kg + 40 g

b) 4.2 ℓ – 270 mℓ

c) 4 kg + 9500 mg

d) 14 km – 2730 m

e) 4 days + 120 hr

2) A bag, which weighs 1.75 kg when empty, is filled with 350 balls, each weighing 180 g. What is the total weight of the full bag (in kg)?

3) John and David live 0.7 km apart. If John takes steps measuring 75 cm, then how many steps would it take him to walk from his house to David's house?

4) A punch recipe calls for 135 mℓ of orange juice, 550 mℓ of sparkling water, and 85 mℓ of apple juice. Is a 1.0 ℓ pitcher big enough to hold the punch? If so, how much more punch could be added. If not, how much will spill?

5) Circle that which is most reasonable.
a) 250 g
   toy truck   pickup truck
                monster truck

b) 6 kg
   golf ball   football   bowling ball

c) 40 km
   sled ride   car ride   airplane ride

d) 1.9 m
   doll's height   person's height
              house's height

e) 15 mℓ
   full spoon   full bowl   full bathtub

f) 400 mℓ
   full spoon   full bowl   full bathtub

6) David can carry 15 bricks, each brick weighing 850 g. How many kg of bricks can David carry at one time?

7) Tom has a book that is, without the cover, 3.2 cm thick. If the book has 800 pages, then how thick is the average leaf, in millimetres? (Remember, each leaf has a page on the front and one on the back.)

8) Complete:
a) 25 days = _____ hr

b) 48 pt = _____ gal

c) 56 mm = _____ cm

d) 97 mℓ = _____ ℓ

e) 75 cm = _____ m

f) 490 min = _____ hr

g) 21 lb = _____ st

h) 1.2 ℓ = _____ mℓ

i) 35,200 mg = _____ kg

j) 15 min = _____ s

k) 8¼ kg = _____ g

l) 30 km = _____ m

Mental arithmetic

9) $44 \times 25 =$

10) $25 \times 16 =$

11) $25 \times 14 =$

12) $31 \times 29 =$

13) $13 \times 15 =$

14) $54 \div 10,000 =$

15) $26 \times 11 =$

16) $16 \times 999 =$

Review

17) *Division.* Leave your answer as a mixed number.

   a) $8908 \div 29$

   b) $86{,}218 \div 3193$

18) $\sqrt{81}$

19) $\sqrt{8{,}100{,}000{,}000}$

20) $\sqrt[4]{81}$

21) $\sqrt[4]{8{,}100{,}000{,}000}$

22) Convert to an improper fraction:
$15\frac{2}{15}$

23) Convert to a mixed number:
$\dfrac{8908}{29}$

24) The previous problem is the same as which other problem on this sheet?

25) Convert to a mixed number:
$$\dfrac{5\frac{4}{7}}{3\frac{3}{5}}$$

26) Give your answer as both a decimal and as a fraction:
$3.75 + 5\frac{7}{8}$

Measurement – Sheet 4

Add or subtract

1) Give answer in the smallest unit

a) 17.34 m – 784 cm

b) 25 ℓ – 480 mℓ

c) 14 kg – 750 g

d) 75 cm + 18 mm

e) 0.54 ℓ – 26 mℓ

f) $\frac{7}{12}$ hr + 17 min + 480 s

g) 4 m + 18 mm

h) 1500 kg + 2 tonnes

2) A loaf of bread, weighing 972 g, is cut into 18 equal slices. What is the weight of each slice?

3) A bag, which weighs 50 g when empty, has 600 identical marbles in it. If the full bag weighs 1.40 kg, then what is the weight of one marble?

4) Two lines are drawn on a chalkboard. The first line is 1.65 m long and the second is 185 cm long. Which line is longer, and by how much?

5) 1 ℓ of water has a weight of 1 kg. What is the weight of 573,000 mℓ of water?

6) Circle the measurement that makes the most sense.

a) Width of a chalkboard

   2.5 m   2.5 cm

b) Weight of a shoe

   4 kg   450 g

c) Volume of balloon
2 ℓ   45 mℓ

d) Diameter of a pizza
48 cm   1.8 m

7) Complete:
a) 2 days = _____ min

b) 50 fl oz = _____ pints

c) 37 g = _____ kg

d) 300 m = _____ cm

e) 26 mℓ = _____ ℓ

f) 80 fl oz = _____ gal

g) 5690 ℓ = _____ mℓ

h) 3.5 m = _____ mm

i) 158,840 cm = _____ km

j) 2708 mg = _____ g

k) 316 tonne = _____ kg

l) 1200 mm = _____ km

8) A window washer is washing a 25 m tall building. He has four buckets of cleaning solution, each one holding 4.5 ℓ.
a) He wants to reach a window that is 1530 cm above the ground. How far will the window washer have to lower himself from the roof to reach the window?

b) There are 240 windows that need to be washed and the average window takes 25 mℓ of cleaning solution. How much cleaning solution will be left after all the windows have been washed?

Mental arithmetic
9) $25 \times 36 =$

10) $320 \times 25 =$

11) $1.8 \times 25 =$

12) $19 \times 21 =$

13) $19 \times 17 =$

14) $6.4 \div 4 =$

15) $700 \times 300 =$

16) $6 \times 9999 =$

Review
17) *Divisibility.* State whether each number is evenly divisible by anything from 2 to 12 (but not 7).

a) 4,568,212

b) 31,640,625

18) Convert to a decimal.

a) $\dfrac{5}{6}$

b) $\dfrac{5}{60}$

c) $\dfrac{389}{1111}$

19) $\left(2\dfrac{1}{5}\right)^2$

20) $\left(2\dfrac{1}{5}\right)^3$

21) *Challenge*

$$\dfrac{\dfrac{5}{3\frac{3}{4}}}{5\frac{1}{2}-\dfrac{5}{2-\frac{\frac{1}{2}}{4}}}$$

Measurement – Sheet 5

Add or subtract

1) Give answer in the largest unit:

a) $45\,\ell + 270\,\text{m}\ell =$

b) $4300\,\text{g} + 87\,\text{kg} =$

c) $5\,\text{yd} - 30\,\text{in} =$

d) $3\,\text{m} + 20\,\text{cm} - 360\,\text{mm} =$

e) $0.4\,\text{m} + 763\,\text{cm} =$

2) Complete:

a) ¾ mi = _____ yd

b) ⅜ ℓ = _____ mℓ

c) 1.5 cm = _____ mm

d) 9706 cm = _____ km

e) 1½ gal = _____ fl oz

f) 84 mm = _____ m

g) 1 week = _____ hr

h) 73.1 kg = _____ g

i) 300 mℓ = _____ ℓ

j) 49 lb = _____ st

k) 6700 mm = _____ m

l) 8.1 kg = _____ mg

m) 1 hr = _____ s

n) 144 pt = _____ gal

3) A crate loaded with 36 blocks of wood
    weighs 1.43 tonnes. Each block weighs
    37.5 kg. What does the crate weigh
    when empty? (Give your answer in kg.)

4) 2 ℓ of a certain paint will cover 25 sq m
    How many litres of paint are needed to
    cover 300 sq m?

5) A certain relay race is made up of 8 seg-
    ments. Each segment is 1500 m long.
a) How long is the whole race (in km)?

b) What fraction of the race has passed
    after 3000 m?

c) How many complete segments have
    been finished after 7600 m?

d) Jane drinks an average of 325 mℓ
    during each segment. If she ran all
    segments, how many litres would she
    drink during the whole race?

e) If she started with 3.0 ℓ, how much is
    left at the end of the race (in mℓ)?

Mental arithmetic
6) $65^2 =$

7) $35^2 =$

8) $120 \times 25 =$

9) $25 \times 28 =$

10) $51 \times 490 =$

11) $216 \div 5 =$

12) $103 \times 105 =$

13) $2800 \times 25 =$

Review

14) *Short division.* Leave your answer as a mixed number:

$432{,}503 \div 6$

15) Convert to a fraction.
   a) 0.089

   b) 0.375

   c) 0.0025

16) Reduce $\dfrac{3888}{8208}$

17) $\dfrac{3}{11} + \dfrac{5}{6}$

18) Multiply out only the first two, and then look for patterns for the rest.
   a) $12{,}345{,}679 \times 18 =$

b) $12{,}345{,}679 \times 45 =$

c) $12{,}345{,}679 \times 72 =$

d) $12{,}345{,}679 \times 9 =$

e) $12{,}345{,}679 \times 81 =$

f) $12{,}345{,}679 \times 54 =$

g) $12{,}345{,}679 \times 27 =$

h) $12{,}345{,}679 \times 36 =$

i) $12{,}345{,}679 \times 63 =$

Challenge

19) $12{,}345{,}679 \times 999{,}999{,}999 =$

A Student's Workbook for Mathematics in Class 7

Measurement – Sheet 6

1) State what each prefix means
a) kilo-

b) milli-

c) centi-

2) A truck is carrying 1.8 tonnes of metal bars. Each bar has a weight of 7500 g and a length of 350 cm. If they were all laid end-to-end, then how long would the line of bars be? (Give your answer both in metres and in km)

Add or subtract
3) Give answer in the largest unit:
a) 25 cm + 18 m =

b) 7.3 ℓ – 28 mℓ =

c) 4200 mm + 15 m =

d) 17 min – 510 s =

4) A jug that can hold 1.6 ℓ is ⅝ full. How many mℓ are in the jug?

5) How many 15 g servings are in a 0.42 kg block of cheese?

6) How many 15 mm-thick slices can a 25.5 cm-long loaf of bread be cut into?

7) Circle that which is most reasonable.
a) 2.2 m
length of an arm   length of a bed
length of a football field

b) 1200 kg
weight of a bicycle   weight of a car
weight of a train

c) 384,400 km
distance to town   distance to the moon
distance from Europe to Australia

d) 5 mℓ
volume of a bucket
volume of a mug
volume of a thimble

e) 90 kg
weight of a heavy dog
weight of a heavy horse
weight of a heavy whale

Mental arithmetic
8) $35^2 =$

9) $95^2 =$

10) $850^2 =$

11) $250 \times 4800 =$

12) $160 \div 240 =$

13) $0.014 \div 4 =$

14) $54 \times 11 =$

15) $112 \times 108 =$

16) Complete:
 a) 12 m = _____ cm

 b) 544 ml = _____ l

 c) 0.06 ml = _____ l

 d) 0.097 kg = _____ mg

 e) 38 gal = _____ pt

 f) 0.07 mm = _____ km

 g) 9.34 kg = _____ mg

 h) 16,000 oz = _____ st

 i) 3.8 mg = _____ kg

 j) 5½ l = _____ ml

 k) 1 fl oz = _____ pt

 l) 648 in = _____ yd

Review
17) Roots
 a) $\sqrt{1,000,000}$

 b) $\sqrt[3]{1,000,000}$

 c) $\sqrt[6]{1,000,000}$

 d) $\sqrt[3]{27,000,000}$

 e) $\sqrt[5]{3,200,000}$

18) Convert to a decimal number:
 a) $\frac{1}{8}$

 b) $\frac{725}{999}$

 c) $\frac{7}{50}$

 d) $\frac{71}{88}$

19) Convert to a mixed number:
 a) $\frac{39}{7}$

 b) $\frac{6841}{23}$

20) Convert to an improper fraction:
 a) $8\frac{7}{12}$

 b) $1010\frac{1}{11}$

 c) $3030\frac{3}{11}$

 d) $707,070\frac{7}{11}$

21) Give your answer both as a decimal and as a fraction:
 a) $0.8 - ¾$

 b) $\frac{7}{20} + 0.35$

 c) What is ⅗ of 0.17?

22) $(0.004)^3$

23) $6 \div 8¼$

24) *Challenge*

$$\cfrac{5}{5 + \cfrac{5}{5 + \cfrac{5}{5 + \frac{5}{5}}}}$$

Measurement – Sheet 7

Add or subtract

1) Give answer in the smallest unit:

a) 426 g + 972 mg =

b) 0.023 km + 375 cm =

c) 4.2 ℓ – 976 mℓ =

2) What is ³⁄₁₀ of 50 kg in grams?

3) **Unit cost**

a) Bananas cost £1.35 per kilogram. What is the cost of 12 kg of bananas?

b) A 34 m length of rope costs £25.50. What is the cost per metre?

4) Complete

a) 5 cm = _____ km

b) 0.2 cm = _____ m

c) 0.65 km = _____ m

d) 3 gal = _____ pt

e) 10 pt = _____ gal

f) 84 mg = _____ g

g) 1344 oz = _____ lb

h) 9760 mm = _____ km

i) 473 mℓ = _____ ℓ

j) 4¾ pt = _____ fl oz

k) 6240 min = _____ day

l) 5.26 kg = _____ mg

5) A crate of apples has a weight of 230 kg. When empty, the crate has a weight of 14 kg. An average apple has a weight of 450 g. How many apples are in the crate?

6) A certain car's tank can hold 45 ℓ of petrol. The same car can travel 480 km on a full tank (on the motorway). How far can the car go on one litre of petrol?

7) A human pyramid is made up of people standing on each other's shoulders. The top row has one person, the second row has two and so on. Each person is 1.8 m tall, and the distance from their shoulders to the top of their head is 30 cm.
a) How tall would a 45-person pyramid be?

b) How many people would be in a pyramid that is 6.3 m tall?

Mental arithmetic
8) $700 \div 25 =$

9) $350 \div 25 =$

10) $825 \div 25 =$

11) $45^2 =$

12) $115^2 =$

13) $44 \times 25 =$

14) $26 \times 5 =$

15) $8 \times 99 =$

Review
16) *Divisibility.* State whether each number is evenly divisible by anything from 2 to 12 (but not 7):

a) 381,250

b) 6,852,318

17) *Roots*

a) $\sqrt{49,000,000}$

b) $\sqrt{25,600}$

c) $\sqrt[4]{256}$

d) $\sqrt{784}$

18) Convert to a fraction:
a) 0.001

b) 0.42

c) 0.008

19) *Division.* Leave your answer as an exact decimal (perhaps repeating)
$34.1 \div 600$

20) *Challenge*
$410 \div 0.0259$

Ratios I – Sheet 1

1) Find the ratio of milk to water:
a) 4 cups of milk and 6 cups of water.

b) 6 cups of milk and 4 cups of water.

c) 6 cups of water and 4 cups of milk.

d) ½ gal of milk and 3 pints of water.

e) ½ gal of water and 28 fl oz of milk.

f) 240 mℓ of milk and 180 mℓ of water.

2) What is the ratio of Jane's to Larry's to Kevin's money if they have £24, £32 and £44, respectively?

3) For each problem, give the ratio of Bill's to Mary's:
a) What is the ratio of their weights if Bill weighs 72 kg and Mary weighs 64 kg?

b) What would the ratio of their weights be if they were weighed in lb?

c) What is the ratio of their heights if Bill is 5 ft 4 in tall and Mary is 5 ft 8 in tall?

d) What would the ratio of their heights be if they were measured in metres?

e) What is the ratio of their pay if Bill gets paid £5/hr and Mary gets paid £150/week? (Both of them work 40 hours per week.)

4) Which of the following classes at a school have equal ratios of boys to girls?
· Class One has 18 boys and 12 girls.

· Class Two has 10 boys and 8 girls.

· Class Three has 15 girls and 12 boys.

· Class Four has 12 girls and 15 boys.

· Class Five has 13 boys and 9 girls.

· Class Six has 15 boys and 10 girls.

5) Redraw each figure according to the given instructions. Each drawing should be sketched carefully by hand, but without a ruler.

a) Reduce the triangle to 75%, and mirror it about a horizontal line.

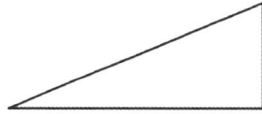

b) Reduce the triangle to 40%, mirror it about a vertical line and rotate it clockwise by 90°.

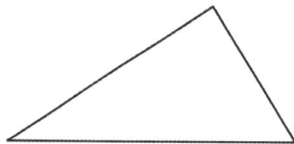

c) Enlarge the figure to 150%, mirror it about a horizontal line and rotate it clockwise by 180°.

6) With the previous problems, you had to reduce or enlarge a figure. If we put a figure in a photocopier and reduce or enlarge it, then the resulting figure and the original figure are said to be similar to one another, such as these two figures here:

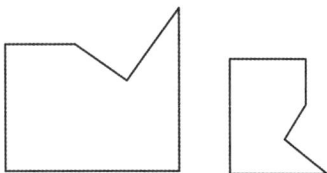

What can we say that is true about any pair of similar figures?

Mental arithmetic

7) $15 \times 70 =$

8) $220 \times 15 =$

9) $14 \times 15 =$

10) $90 \div 25 =$

11) $75^2 =$

12) $25 \times 360 =$

13) $225 \times 4 =$

14) $7024 - 2989 =$

Review

15) $0.6 \text{ cm} = \underline{\hspace{1cm}} \text{ km}$

16) $5280 \text{ yd} = \underline{\hspace{1cm}} \text{ mi}$

17) $40 \text{ fl oz} = \underline{\hspace{1cm}} \text{ pt}$

18) $1.3 \text{ km} = \underline{\hspace{1cm}} \text{ cm}$

19) $\dfrac{6\frac{2}{3}}{4}$

20) $\dfrac{48}{49} \times \dfrac{35}{36}$

21) *Division.* Leave the answer as an exact decimal (perhaps repeating): $0.9218 \div 0.006$

22) $(0.0052)^2$

Ratios I – Sheet 2

1) Janet is 135 cm tall and weighs 40 kg, and Maria is 150 cm tall and weighs 60 kg.
a) What is the ratio of Maria's weight to Janet's weight?

b) What is the ratio of Janet's weight to Maria's weight?

c) What is the ratio of Janet's height to Maria's height?

2) Reduce each ratio:
a) $10:5$

b) $15:25$

c) $6:10$

d) $36:4$

e) $84:108$

f) $1716:1584$

3) What is the ratio of water to flour in a recipe that calls for:
a) 500 mℓ of water and 750 mℓ of flour?

b) 5 eggs, 1 ℓ of flour and 500 mℓ of water?

c) 1.25 ℓ of water, 250 mℓ of milk and 500 mℓ of flour?

d) 625 mℓ of flour and 0.625 ℓ of water?

4) *Proportions as a fraction*
a) 8 is what proportion of 24?

b) 200 is what proportion of 500?

c) 35 is what proportion of 56?

d) 4 is what proportion of 7?

e) 8 is what proportion of 5?

5) What can be said about any two similar figures?

6) Is each statement true or false?
a) All squares are similar.

b) All rectangles are similar.

c) All pentagons are similar.

d) All regular pentagons are similar.

e) All circles are similar.

7) State whether each pair of figures is definitely similar or not. (Not drawn to scale.)

a)

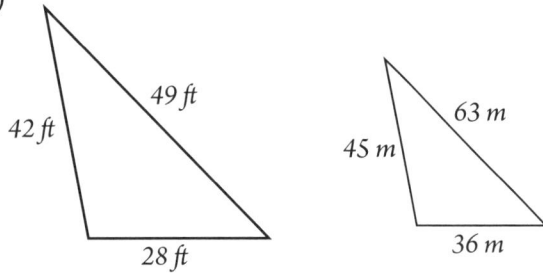

b)

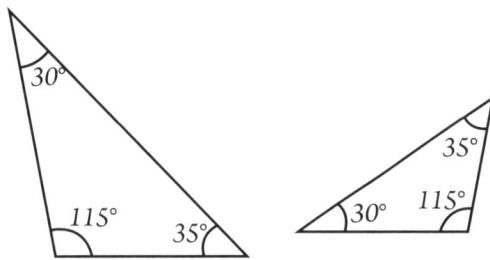

c)

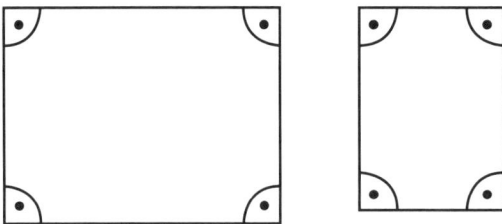

d)

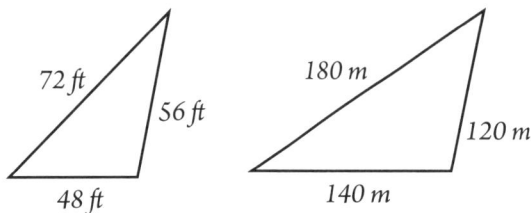

8) Which one of these triangles is not similar to the others? (Not drawn to scale.)

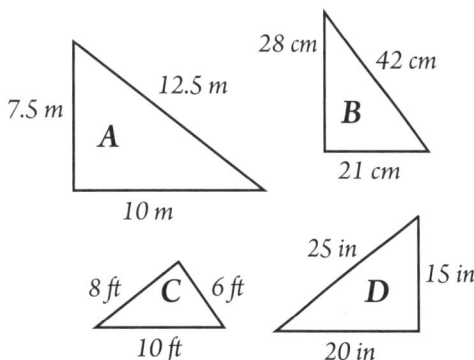

The three thoughts of a ratio

What does it mean to say that the ratio of girls to boys in a group is 5 to 3?

$$G : B = 5 : 3$$

We can associate three thoughts with the above ratio:

1. $3\,G = 5\,B$

In words, this means that 3 times the number of girls is equal to 5 times the number of boys.

2. $B = \dfrac{3}{5}\,G$

In words, this means that the number of boys is equal to ⅗ the number of girls.

3. $G = \dfrac{5}{3}\,B$

In words, this means that the number of girls is equal to ⅝ the number of boys.

We will use these three 'thoughts' to solve ratio problems.

Example: The ratio of girls to boys in a group is 5 to 3. How many girls are there, if there are 21 boys?

Solution (for Class Seven): We first think of the three thoughts given above, and then recognise that the third one will help us in finding the answer to the question because it tells us how to calculate the number of girls. Specifically, it says that the number of girls is ⅝ of the number of boys. So we do ⅝ times 21 to get an answer of 35.

Note: This method of solving the problem requires a good understanding of what a ratio is. The typical algebraic solution (i.e. G is to 21 as 5 is to 3), which has us set up the equation

$$\frac{G}{21} = \frac{5}{3}$$

requires no real understanding of ratios, and is therefore not done until Class Eight.

9) Bill has £36 and Jack has £45.
a) What is the ratio of Bill's money to Jack's money?

b) What are the three thoughts associated with this ratio? Write each thought both as an equation and as a sentence.

10) The ratio of Jeff's money to Patty's money is 2 to 3. $(J:P = 2:3)$. How much money does Jeff have if Patty has £78? (*Hint:* see the example.)

Mental arithmetic

11) $15 \times 180 =$

12) 15% of $240 =$

13) 15% of $62 =$

14) $120 \div 25 =$

15) $4000 \div 25 =$

16) $95^2 =$

17) $287 \div 999 =$

18) $13{,}000 \div 5 =$

Review

19) Is 36,082,717 evenly divisible by 11?

Ratios I – Sheet 3

1) Consider these figures:

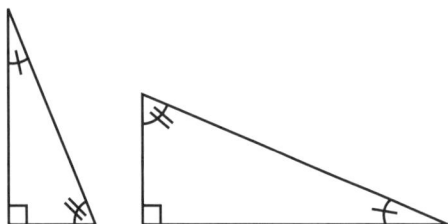

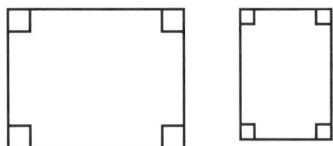

a) Are the two triangles definitely similar?

b) Are the two rectangles definitely similar?

c) A triangle has sides of length 10 m, 24 m and 26 m. Give the lengths of the sides of any other triangle that is similar to it.

d) A rectangle has a 10 cm base and an 8 cm height. Give the dimensions of any other rectangle that is similar to it.

2) Is each statement true or false?
a) All triangles are similar.

b) All isosceles triangles are similar.

c) All equilateral triangles are similar.

d) All equiangular hexagons are similar.

e) All equilateral hexagons are similar.

f) All regular hexagons are similar.

g) All circles are similar.

3) Give the reciprocal:
a) ¾

b) ⅑

c) ⁵⁄₃

d) 2⅜

e) 3

Give the reciprocal as a decimal:
f) 0.3

g) 2.2

4) Given that the ratio of milk to water is 3 to 5 $(M:W = 3:5)$
a) How much milk is needed for 1.5 ℓ of water?

b) How much water is needed for 150 mℓ of milk?

5) What is the ratio of flour to water, given:

a) 2 ℓ of water and 2500 mℓ of flour?

b) ½ ℓ of flour and 750 mℓ of water?

c) 1.1 ℓ of water and 650 mℓ of flour?

A Student's Workbook for Mathematics in Class 7

6) **Proportions as a fraction**
a) 160 is what proportion of 240?

b) 240 is what proportion of 160?

c) 1.25 is what proportion of 1.75?

d) 1.75 is what proportion of 1.25?

7) In a class of 10 girls and 15 boys:
a) What is the ratio of girls to boys?

b) What proportion of the class is girls?

c) What proportion of the class is boys?

8) Look at *The three thoughts of a ratio* in the previous worksheet. Given a ratio of girls to boys that is equal to 7 to 4 $(G:B = 7:4)$:
a) What are the three thoughts associated with this ratio? Write each thought both as an equation and as a sentence.

b) If there are 56 girls, then how many boys are there?

c) If there are 56 boys, then how many girls are there?

d) If there are 121 girls and boys combined, then how many boys are there?

9) The ratio of Gabe's height to Nancy's height is 6 to 5 $(G:N = 6:5)$.
a) What are the three thoughts (as equations only) associated with this ratio?

b) What is Gabe's height if Nancy's is 1.75 m?

c) What is Nancy's height if Gabe's is 1.56 m?

d) What is Nancy's height if Gabe's is 69 in?

10) Give the ratio of the base to the height.

a)

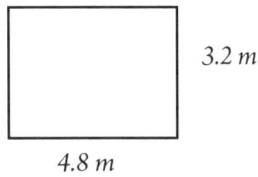

3.2 m

4.8 m

b)

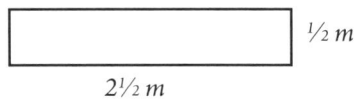

½ m

2½ m

Mental arithmetic

11) $12 \times 45 =$

12) $35 \times 80 =$

13) $55 \times 240 =$

14) 15% of £28 =

15) $48{,}000 \div 1{,}200 =$

16) $2300 \times 11 =$

17) $90 \div 150 =$

18) $107^2 =$

Review

19) 25 fl oz = _____ pt

20) 13.7 g = _____ mg

21) 0.04 cm = _____ mm

22) 5000 kg = _____ tonne

23) 3.4 cm = _____ mm

24) 7 mm = _____ m

25) 300 in = _____ yd

26) 50 ℓ = _____ mℓ

Ratios I – Sheet 4

1) Given that a recipe calls for 200 mℓ of flour and 500 mℓ of water ($F : W = 2 : 5$), and you want to enlarge the amount:

a) How much water is needed for 400 mℓ of flour?

b) How much water is needed for 800 mℓ of flour?

c) How much flour is needed for 800 mℓ of water?

d) How much flour is needed for 625 mℓ of water?

e) How much water is needed for 250 mℓ of flour?

2) At a shop selling baseball bats the ratio of aluminium bats to wooden bats is 5 to 2 (A : W = 5 : 2).

a) Write down the three thoughts associated with this ratio. Write each thought both as an equation and as a sentence.

b) If they have 40 wooden bats, then how many are aluminium?

c) If they have 50 aluminium bats, then how many are wooden?

d) What proportion of the bats is aluminium?

e) What proportion of the bats is wooden?

f) If they have a total of 63 bats, then how many are aluminium and how many are wooden?

3) The ratio of boys to girls in a group is 5 to 4.

a) If there are 270 boys, then how many girls are there?

b) If there are 36 girls, then how many boys are there?

c) If there are 630 girls and boys combined, then how many are boys and how many are girls?

4) Find X given that each pair of rectangles is similar.

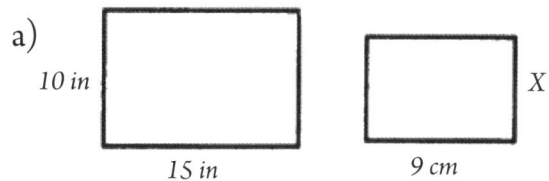

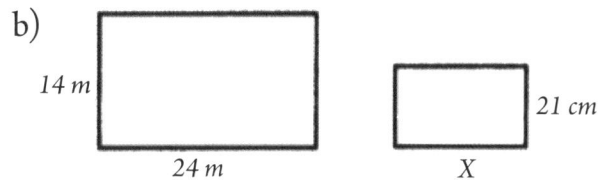

a)

10 in   15 in   9 cm   X

b)

14 m   24 m   21 cm   X

c)

14 m   24 m   21 cm   X

Two forms of a ratio

Using the example that Jeff has £25 and Meg has £20. We can express the ratio of their money in two ways:

Whole number form
This is what we have been using until now. Both numbers in the ratio must be *whole numbers*.

With the above example, we express the ratio as

$$J : M = 5 : 4$$

It has three thoughts associated with it:
1. $5\,M = 4\,J$
2. $J = \frac{5}{4}\,M$
3. $M = \frac{4}{5}\,J$

Decimal form
The first number is often a decimal, and *the second number must be 1.*

With the above example, we divide 4 into 5 in order to express the ratio as

$$J : M = 1.25 : 1$$

It has two thoughts associated with it:
1. $J = 1.25 \times M$

which means that J is 1.25 times as big as M.
2. $M = J \div 1.25$

which means that M is 1.25 times smaller than J.

Alternatively, we could have divided 5 into 4, which would have given us the ratio as

$$M : J = 0.8 : 1$$

With this ratio, the two thoughts are:
1. $M = 0.8 \times J$

which means that M is 0.8 times as big as J.
2. $J = M \div 0.8$

which means that J is 0.8 times smaller than M. (Which results in J being larger than M.)

5) At a college there are 120 first year students, 150 second year, 125 third year and 128 fourth year students.
a) Give the ratio of first year to second year students in whole number form.

b) Give the three thoughts associated with the ratio that you gave above.

c) Give the ratio of second year to first year students in whole number form.

d) Give the three thoughts associated with the ratio that you gave above.

e) Give the ratio of second year to third year sudents in decimal form.

f) Give the two thoughts associated with the ratio that you gave above.

g) Give the ratio of third year to second year students in decimal form.

h) Give the two thoughts associated with the ratio that you gave above.

6) Give the reciprocal:
a) ⅗

b) ²⁄₉

c) ⁹⁄₂

d) 3½

e) 7

Give the reciprocals as decimals:
f) 0.4

g) 3.2

7) Give the reciprocal:
a) $X : Y = 7 : 15$

b) $A : B = 3 : 2$

c) $G : L = 17 : 22$

d) $H : J = 1.8 : 1$

e) $E : Q = 0.625 : 1$

Ratios I – Sheet 5

1) Beth has £360 and Frank has £150.
a) What is the ratio of Beth's money to Frank's money in whole number form?

b) Give the three thoughts associated with the above ratio.

c) What is the ratio of Frank's money to Beth's money in whole number form?

d) Give the three thoughts associated with the above ratio.

e) What is the ratio of Beth's money to Frank's money in decimal form?

f) Give the two thoughts associated with the above ratio.

g) What is the ratio of Frank's money to Beth's money in decimal form?

h) Give the two thoughts associated with this ratio.

2) Give the reciprocal of each ratio.
a) B : G = 7 : 5

b) H : D = 2 : 7

c) Y : X = 2.5 : 1

d) X : Y = 0.4 : 1

3) Convert each ratio from whole number form to decimal form.

a) B : G = 7 : 5

b) H : D = 8 : 3

4) Convert each ratio from decimal form to whole number form.
a) X : Z = 4.3 : 1

b) K : J = 3.25 : 1

5) Find *X* given that each pair of figures is similar.
a)

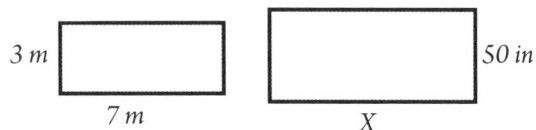

3 m

7 m

50 in

X

b)

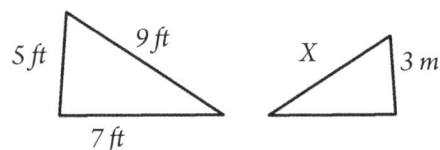

5 ft   9 ft   X   3 m

7 ft

6) On Jill's farm the ratio of cows to goats is 5 to 13. (C : G = 5 : 13)
a) Give the three thoughts associated with this ratio.

b) If there are 35 cows, then how many goats are there?

c) If there are 52 goats, then how many cows are there?

d) If there are 540 cows and goats combined, then how many are cows and how many are goats?

7) A recipe calls for 1,250 mℓ of milk and 3,750 mℓ of flour. How much milk is needed if the recipe is enlarged to include 4½ ℓ of flour?

8) In determining the height of a flagpole, Fred measured that the length of the pole's shadow was 15.6 m, and that the length of a 1 metre stick's shadow, when held vertically next to the flagpole, was 160 cm. Calculate the height of the flagpole.

Mental arithmetic

9) $140 \div 35 =$

10) $18 \div 1.5 =$

11) $27 \div 4.5 =$

12) $22 \times 45 =$

13) $55 \times 8 =$

14) $350 \times 180 =$

15) $115,000 \div 25 =$

16) $64 \div 4 =$

Review

17) $0.03 \text{ g} =$ _____ kg

18) $5\frac{1}{2}$ tonne = _____ kg

19) $16 \text{ fl oz} =$ _____ pt

20) $0.85 \text{ mm} =$ _____ cm

21) $\sqrt{14{,}400}$

22) $\sqrt[2]{6{,}250{,}000}$

23) $\sqrt[4]{6{,}250{,}000}$

24) $312\frac{2}{5} - 309\frac{2}{3}$

25) *Division* (leave the answer as a mixed number)
$7000 \div 333$

Ratios I – Sheet 6

1) A recipe for salad dressing calls for ¼ ℓ of oil and 50 mℓ of vinegar.

a) What is the ratio of oil to vinegar in whole number form?

b) What is the ratio of oil to vinegar in decimal form?

c) If the recipe is to be enlarged, how much oil is needed (in ℓ) for 120 mℓ of vinegar?

d) How much vinegar is needed for 650 mℓ of oil?

2) Convert these ratios from whole number form to decimal form (the decimals may repeat):

a) $X:Y = 18:5$

b) $Y:X = 5:18$

3) Convert these ratios from decimal form to whole number form:

a) $X:Y = 3.5:1$

b) $M:K = 0.32:1$

4) The ratio of boys to girls in Jeff's class is 3 to 2. $(B:G = 3:2)$

a) If there are 18 girls, then how many boys are there?

b) What proportion of the class is boys?

c) What proportion of the class is girls?

d) If there are 30 students in the class, then how many are girls and how many are boys?

5) A litre of milk is poured into two jugs such that the ratio of their volumes is 3 to 5. How much milk is in each pitcher (in mℓ)?

6) Write the four ways to express the ratio of this rectangle's dimensions.

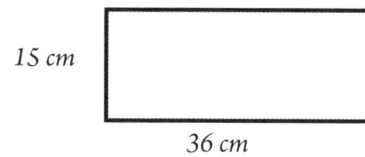

15 cm

36 cm

7) Find X given that these two triangles are similar.

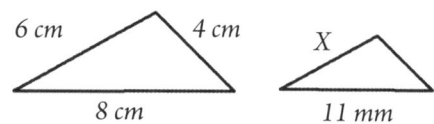

6 cm   4 cm X

8 cm   11 mm

8) Find X and Y given that the triangles are similar.

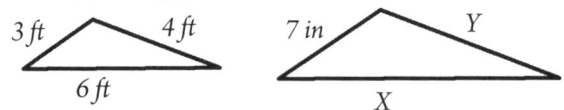

3 ft   4 ft   7 in Y

6 ft X

9) On a certain train, the ratio of first class seats to second class seats is 3 to 7.

a) If there are 210 first class seats, then how many second class seats are there?

b) If there are 210 second class seats, then how many first class seats are there?

c) If there are a total of 210 seats, then how many are second and how many are first class?

Review

10) $\frac{3}{4} - \frac{11}{18}$

11) $5\frac{2}{5} \times 1\frac{7}{8}$

12) $5\frac{2}{5} \div 1\frac{7}{8}$

13) What is $\frac{2}{5}$ of $6\frac{1}{4}$?

14) *The shadow problem*

Choose a narrow, tall (at least 3 m) object outside to calculate the height of (e.g. a tree or a telephone pole). At a moment when there is sun, measure the length of the object's shadow. Take a long pole (or a stick) and measure its height and the length of its shadow when held vertically next to the tall object.

Now, draw two triangles – one for the tall object and one for the pole – roughly to scale. With each triangle, the horizontal side represents the length of a shadow, the vertical side represents the height and the third side (which won't be used) represents the line that could be drawn from the top of the object to the end of its shadow. Label these triangles with the lengths that you measured and label the height of the object (which is what you are trying to calculate) as *X*. Calculate the height of the object. Round your answer to three significant figures.

Ratios I – Sheet 7

1) Find *X* and *Y* given that the two figures are similar.

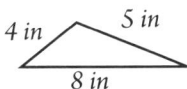

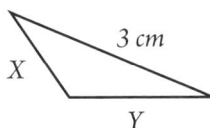

2) Barry has £21.00 and Ned has £21.60. Give the ratio of Barry's money to Ned's money:

a) In whole number form.

b) In decimal form.

3) Give the reciprocal of each ratio:
a) B : G = 11 : 5

b) H : D = 3 : 13

c) R : W = 0.9 : 1

d) X : Y = 3.6 : 1

4) Convert this ratio to decimal form:
B : G = 13 : 4

5) Convert this ratio to whole number form:
H : D = 2.125 : 1

6) Two litres of milk is poured into three jugs such that the ratio of their volumes is 3 : 5 : 8. How much milk is in each jug (in mℓ)?

7) How can £550 be split between four people in a ratio of 5 : 3 : 2 : 1?

8) The length of a shadow of a tree is 7.5 m. A 1.5 metre pole next to it has a shadow 75 cm long. How tall is the tree?

9) Write the four ways to express the ratio of this rectangle's dimensions.

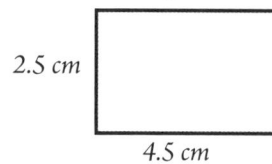

2.5 cm

4.5 cm

10) An amount of money is to be divided between Mary and John in a ratio of 7 : 5.
a) How much does John get if Mary gets £28?

b) How much does Mary get if John gets £45?

c) How much does each person get if there is a total of £360?

11) Find X given that each pair of figures is similar.

a)

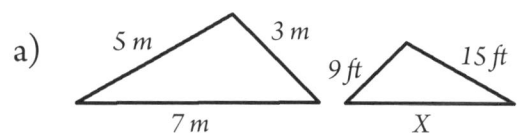

5 m   3 m
9 ft   15 ft
7 m   X

b)

4.9 m
2.6 m $3\frac{1}{4}$ in   X

12) Given that the ratio of cows to goats on a farm is 9 to 2 (C : G = 9 : 2)

a) What are the three thoughts associated with this ratio? Write each thought both as an equation and as a sentence.

b) If there are 198 goats, then how many cows are there?

c) If there are 198 cows, then how many goats are there?

d) If there are 198 goats and cows combined, then how many are goats and how many are cows?

Review

13) *Short Division.* Leave the answer as an exact decimal (perhaps repeating):

$748.4 \div 0.09$

14) $\left(3\frac{1}{8}\right)^2$

15) $3\frac{5}{6} \times 100$

16) $57\frac{2}{5} - 54\frac{7}{8}$

17) $320.4 - 5.13$

18) 0.008×0.005

Percents – Sheet 1

1) Convert each percentage into both a fraction and a decimal:
a) 21%

b) 25%

c) 50%

d) 53%

e) 7%

f) 5%

2) What is 75%
a) as a decimal?

b) as a fraction?

3) Using your answers from the previous problem, solve the following problem in two ways.
What is 75% of 4800?

4) For each, state whether it is easier to solve the problem by converting the percentage into a fraction or into a decimal, and then solve it.
a) What is 21% of 300?

b) What is 25% of 360?

c) What is 7% of 2930?

d) What is 5% of 1600?

5) Convert 0.37 to a percentage.

6) Explain what you did to get the previous answer, and *why* it worked.

7) Convert to a percentage:
a) ¾

b) ⅖

c) ⁹⁄₁₀

d) ²⁹⁄₁₀₀

8) Explain why the last problem was so easy to do.

9) Convert into a percentage:
a) 0.63

b) 0.95

c) 0.03

d) ¼

e) $^{47}/_{100}$

f) $^{7}/_{100}$

g) $^{53}/_{160}$

10) Explain why the last problem was the most difficult.

Mental arithmetic

11) $34 \times 36 =$

12) $58 \times 52 =$

13) $73 \times 77 =$

14) $210 \div 3.5 =$

15) $1800 \div 45 =$

16) $105 \div 15 =$

17) $80 \times 0.55 =$

18) 15% of £44 =

Review

19) 92 m = _____ km

20) 528,000 mm = _____ m

21) 987 cm = _____ m

22) 0.007 km = _____ cm

23) 320 mg = _____ g

24) 400 fl oz = _____ pt

25) 4.3 kg = _____ mg

26) 0.04 mℓ = _____ ℓ

27) 0.04 ℓ = _____ mℓ

28) 0.31g = _____ kg

29) 3½ lb = _____ oz

30) Give the reciprocal:
a) A : B = 7 : 2

b) G : L = 19 : 22

c) H : J = 4.5 : 1

31) 2.4 ℓ of milk are poured into two jugs such that the ratio of their volumes is 5 : 3. How much milk is in each jug (in mℓ)?

32) $\left(8\frac{4}{7}\right)^2$

33) $\left(8\frac{4}{7}\right)^3$

34) $2\frac{2}{5} + 1\frac{7}{8}$

Percents – Sheet 2

1) First, look through the problems, and then circle those that are easy. Do those in your head. Show your work for the others on a separate sheet.

a) What is 25% of 320?

b) What is 45% of 320?

c) What is 33⅓% of 1800?

d) What is 50% of 72?

e) What is 6% of 79?

f) What is 84% of 619?

g) What is 10% of 619?

h) What is 1% of 43,000?

i) What is 20% of 45?

j) What is 0.35% of 45?

k) What is 125% of 4800?

l) What is 8.1% of 48,000?

2) Try to do each problem by writing it as a fraction, and then changing it into a percent. Divide only if necessary, showing your work on a separate sheet.

a) 24 is what percent of 48?

b) 25 is what percent of 75?

c) 11 is what percent of 90?

d) 700 is what percent of 7000?

e) 140 is what percent of 210?

f) 4500 is what percent of 6000?

g) 35 is what percent of 56?

h) 3500 is what percent of 4200?

i) 527 is what percent of 850?

j) 96 is what percent of 120?

3) Convert into a percent:

a) ³⁄₁₀

b) ¼

c) ⅗

d) ⁷¹⁄₁₀₀

e) ⅓

f) ½

g) ⁹⁄₁₀

h) ³⁄₁₀₀

i) ⅖

j) ⅚

k) ⅞

l) ⅔

m) 0.09

n) 0.3

o) 0.38

p) 0.99

q) 0.8

r) 0.45

4) Convert each percentage into both a fraction and a decimal.

a) 80%

b) 37½%

c) 4%

d) 70%

e) 75%

f) 5%

g) 16⅔%

5) What is:

a) 300 increased by 50%?

b) 300 decreased by 50%?

c) 300 increased by 10%?

d) 300 decreased by 10%?

Mental arithmetic

6) $23 \times 27 =$

7) $81 \times 89 =$

8) $44 \times 46 =$

9) $9000 \div 15 =$

10) $280 \div 3.5 =$

11) $24 \times 45 =$

12) $120 \times 15 =$

13) $3000 \div 25 =$

Review

14) 76 ft = _____ yd

15) $9\ \ell =$ _____ mℓ

16) 0.06 m = _____ mm

17) 9 oz = _____ lb

18) Convert this ratio to decimal form:
B : G = 13 : 5

19) Convert this ratio to whole number form:
H : D = 3.4 : 1

20) A recipe for salad dressing calls for 240 mℓ of oil and 75 mℓ of vinegar.

a) What is the ratio of oil to vinegar in whole number form?

b) What is the ratio of oil to vinegar in decimal form?

c) If the recipe is to be enlarged, how much oil is needed for 450 mℓ of vinegar?

21) How can £216 be split between three people in a ratio of $2:3:4$?

Percents – Sheet 3

1) Convert to a percent (*hint:* try multiplying the numerator and denominator):

a) $\frac{9}{50}$

b) $\frac{11}{20}$

c) $\frac{8}{25}$

d) $\frac{41}{50}$

e) $\frac{87}{100}$

f) $\frac{1}{4}$

g) $\frac{5}{8}$

2) Convert to a percent:

a) 0.61

b) 0.0469

c) 0.003

3) Think fractions!

a) 12 is what percent of 48?

b) 12 is what percent of 24?

c) 12 is what percent of 25?

d) 12 is what percent of 55?

4) Convert to a fraction.

a) 60%

b) 2%

c) 8%

d) 28%

e) $66\frac{2}{3}\%$

f) 30%

g) $83\frac{1}{3}\%$

h) 0.5%

5) What is:
a) 45 increased by 20%?

b) 45 decreased by 20%?

c) 45 increased by 80%?

d) 45 decreased by 80%?

6) First, look through the problems, and then circle those that are easy. Do those in your head. Show your work for the others. What is:
a) 25% of 12?

b) 10% of 800?

c) 1% of 6170?

d) 40% of 55?

e) 25% of 3600?

f) 10% of 37?

g) 87.5% of 240?

h) 13% of 49.6?

i) 0.8% of 3500?

7) *Finding the base*
a) 8 is 50% of what number?

b) 12 is 25% of what number?

c) 13 is 10% of what number?

d) 9 is 1% of what number?

8) A bike is marked at £250, but the newer model costs 7% more. How much does the newer model cost?

9) A bike is priced at £300, but is on sale for a 20% discount. What is the new discounted price?

10) Quickly estimate (do not calculate exactly):
a) What is 48% of 8280?

b) What is 26% of 17.3?

c) 63 is what percent of 92?

d) 3419 is what percent of 7146?

e) £58 is what percent of £62?

Mental arithmetic

11) $53^2 =$

12) $57^2 =$

13) $11{,}000 \div 25 =$

14) $247.5 \div 100 =$

15) $82 \times 88 =$

16) $360 \div 45 =$

17) $350 \times 120 =$

18) $15 \times 320 =$

Review

19) Find X given that the two triangles are similar.

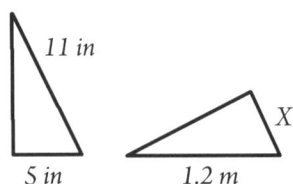

20) The ratio of boys to girls in Jeff's class is $3:4$.

a) If there are 16 girls, then how many boys are there?

b) What proportion of the class is boys?

c) What proportion of the class is girls?

d) If there are 35 students in the class, then how many are boys and how many are girls?

21) Find X given that the two triangles are similar.

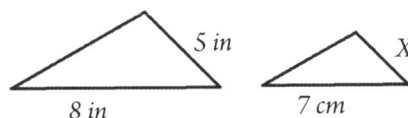

22) An amount of money is to be divided between Mary and John in a ratio of $5:3$. How much does John get if Mary gets £330?

Percents – Sheet 4

1) Convert to a percent (*hint:* try multiplying the numerator and denominator):

a) $^{87}/_{1000}$

b) $^{3}/_{20}$

c) $^{21}/_{25}$

d) $^{1}/_{6}$

e) $^{3}/_{5}$

f) 0.8

g) 0.61

h) 0.08

i) 0.134

2) Convert to a fraction:
a) 35%

b) 20%

c) 62½%

d) 90%

e) 28%

3) Show your work for the problems that you can't do in your head.
a) What is 6% of 13?

b) What is 12.5% of 48?

c) What is 50% of 32?

d) What is 17% of 3200?

e) What is 33⅓% of 3600?

f) What is 300% of 55?

g) What is 5.3% of 200?

h) 12 is what percent of 36?

i) 12 is what percent of 15?

j) 12 is what percent of 32?

k) 12 is what percent of 72?

l) 15 is 20% of what number?

m) 8000 is 25% of what number?

n) 400 is 12½% of what number?

o) What is 80% of 6000?

p) What is 25% of 80?

q) What is 41% of 100?

r) 54 is 40% of what number?

s) 6 is what percent of 60?

t) 9 is what percent of 24?

4) Quickly estimate:
a) What is 11% of 690?

b) What is 36% of 258?

c) £3.08 is what percent of £16.50?

d) What is 82% of 347?

5) *Increase/decrease problems*
a) What is 7000 increased by 6%?

b) What is 7000 decreased by 6%?

c) 16 to 28 is what percentage increase?

6) What do you end up at when 200 is increased by 10% and then that result is decreased by 10%?

7) Surcharge and discount:
a) How much do you have to pay for a shirt marked at £28 if there is a 5% surcharge for special colours?

b) A jacket normally listed for £52.50 is on sale for a 35% discount. What is the new discounted price?

c) In a sale Lenny paid €69.70 for a jacket marked at €82.00. What was the percentage discount?

Mental arithmetic

8) $52^2 =$

9) $59^2 =$

10) $71 \times 79 =$

11) $1800 \div 45 =$

12) 15% of £6200 =

13) $110 \times 107 =$

14) $414 - 395 =$

15) $26 \div 999 =$

Review

16) $\dfrac{7}{80} + \dfrac{11}{120}$

17) $(0.025)^2$

18) *Division* (leave the answer as a mixed number):
$2384 \div 693$

Percents – Sheet 5

Do Problems 1 to 6 in your head!

1) Convert to a percent:

a) ¾

b) ⁷⁄₁₀

c) ⅓

d) ³⁄₂₀

e) ⅚

f) 0.53

g) 0.06

h) 0.045

i) 1.16

2) Convert to a fraction:

a) 40%

b) 66²⁄₃%

c) 13%

d) 37½%

3) Convert to a decimal:

a) 53%

b) 9%

c) 90%

d) 14.37%

4) What is:

a) 10% of 52?

b) 1% of 6000?

c) 50% of 8?

d) 100% of 83.48?

e) 20% of 15?

f) 1% of 463?

g) 62½% of 2400?

h) 83⅓% of 360?

5) *Percentages*

a) 6 is what percent of 12?

b) 4 is what percent of 12?

c) 300 is what percent of 500?

d) 7 is what percent of 700?

e) 10 is what percent of 12?

f) 60 is what percent of 90?

g) 28 is what percent of 35?

6) Quickly estimate:

a) What is 52% of 238?

b) What is 23% of 37?

c) 52 is what percent of 160?

d) £7.20 is what percent of £697?

e) 68.4 is what percent of 71.8?

7) Calculate an exact answer:
a) What is 28% of 58?

b) What is 250% of €8900?

c) 78 is what percent of 650?

d) 2.94 is what percent of 840?

e) 210 is 25% of what number?

f) 210 is 60% of what number?

8) *Increase/decrease problems*
a) What is 72,000 decreased by $62\frac{1}{2}$%?

b) What is 400 increased by 260%?

c) 600 to 800 is what percentage increase?

d) 800 to 600 is what percentage decrease?

e) Why weren't the above two answers the same?

9) Jane borrowed £500 from her neighbour at 8% simple interest. What does she owe, in total, after 3 years?

10) Janet borrowed £500 from a bank at 8% interest compounded annually. What does she owe, in total, after 3 years?

Mental arithmetic

11) $53 \times 47 =$

12) $78 \times 82 =$

13) $61 \times 59 =$

14) $3.1 \div 5 =$

15) $53 \times 57 =$

16) $45 \times 22 =$

17) $210 \div 35 =$

18) $12 \times 99 =$

Review

19) 3.94 mg = _____ g

20) 34.2 mℓ = _____ ℓ

21) 80 cm = _____ mm

22) Give the four ways to express the ratio of this rectangle's dimensions.

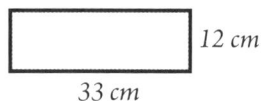

12 cm

33 cm

Percents – Sheet 6

1) Find each answer by using the easiest method possible. Show work on a separate sheet for those problems that can't be done in your head.

a) What is 25% of 140?

b) What is 80% of 450?

c) What is 15% of 220?

d) What is 1% of 741?

e) What is 33⅓% of 1200?

f) What is 83⅓% of 12,000?

g) What is 160% of 25?

h) What is 0.02% of 3000?

i) 8 is what percent of 16?

j) 8 is what percent of 160?

k) 70 is what percent of 210?

l) 31 is what percent of 310?

m) 14 is what percent of 150?

n) 14 is what percent of 16?

o) 71 is 10% of what number?

p) 40 is 20% of what number?

q) 300 is 66⅔% of what number?

r) 78 is 17% of what number?

s) 5022 is 81% of what number?

2) Quickly estimate:
a) What is 71% of 245?

b) What is 9% of 5630?

c) What is 43% of 7?

d) 19 is what percent of 82?

e) 63 is what percent of 130?

f) 8567 is what percent of 9100?

3) What do you end up with if you increase 55 by 40%, and then decrease that result by 40%?

4) Increase and decrease:
a) Going from 5200 up to 6500 is what percentage increase?

b) Going from 6500 down to 5200 is what percentage decrease?

c) Why were the answers to the above two problems different?

5) Including home delivery, Jen paid £213 for a tent that was priced at £200. What was the cost of delivery as a percent?

6) John bought a shirt at a 40% discount that was originally marked at €45. What was the price after the discount?

7) A bank offers a savings account with 2% interest compounded annually. What will be the balance of an account after 5 years, if the initial deposit was £600? (Assume no further activity in the account.)

8) *Challenge*
The discounted price of a bike was £224, and the discount rate was 20%. What was the original price?

Review

9) Reduce $\frac{5175}{17775}$

11) $\dfrac{5\frac{3}{5}}{1\frac{2}{5}}$

10) $42\frac{2}{9} - 38\frac{4}{5}$

Percents – Sheet 7

1) Find each answer by using the easiest method possible. Show work on a separate sheet for those problems that can't be done in your head.

a) What is $12\frac{1}{2}$% of 160?

b) What is 75% of 280?

c) What is 15% of 280?

d) What is 1% of 87?

e) What is $16\frac{2}{3}$% of 1200?

f) What is $87\frac{1}{2}$% of 16?

g) What is 700% of 40?

h) What is 0.58% of 300?

i) 60 is what percent of 150?

j) 52 is what percent of 108?

k) 24 is what percent of 36?

l) 300 is 25% of what?

m) 21 is 6% of what?

2) What is:
a) 72 increased by 2%?

b) 240 decreased by $33\frac{1}{3}$%?

c) 5 increased by 60%?

d) 610 decreased by 4.3%?

3) *Increase and decrease*
a) Going from 80 up to 90 is what percentage increase?

b) Going from 90 up to 100 is what percentage increase?

c) Going from 100 down to 90 is what percent decrease?

d) Going from 400 down to 325 is what percentage decrease?

4) Calculate an exact answer:
a) What is 38% of 410?

b) What is 420% of £700?

c) 3500 is what percent of 4200?

d) 2 is what percent of 7500?

e) 120 is $33\frac{1}{3}$% of what number?

f) 90 is $37\frac{1}{2}$% of what number?

5) A tent normally listed for £480 is on sale for a 35% discount. What is the new discounted price?

6) Larry borrowed £2,000 from a bank at 7% interest compounded annually. What does he owe, in total, after 4 years?

7) A bike, originally priced at £480, was sold at a discount for £345.60. What was the percentage discount rate?

8) *Challenge*

Calculating the cost of driving.

a) John bought a new car for £39,000 and then sold it for £20,000 two years later. By what percentage has the value depreciated (i.e. decreased)?

b) Over those two years, what was the total operating cost and the cost per km given that he spent:
   • £750 per year on insurance
   • £450 a year on repairs and maintenance an average of £220 monthly for interest payments
   • £850 annually for other costs (parking, tolls, tax, etc.)
   and drove it 20,000 km per year?
   (Use 8 ℓ/100 km for petrol usage, and £1.20/ℓ for the cost of petrol. Don't forget about the depreciation cost from part a!)

c) Petrol was what percent of the total operating cost for the two years? (Rounded to three significant figures.)

Ratios II – Sheet 1

1) The ratio of Gabe's hourly wage to Nancy's hourly wage is 7 to 9.
   $(G : N = 7 : 9)$

a) What are the three thoughts (as equations only) associated with this ratio?

b) What is Gabe's hourly wage if Nancy's is £13.50/hr?

c) What is Nancy's hourly wage if Gabe's is £9.10/hr?

2) Which of these figures are similar.
   (Not drawn to scale.)

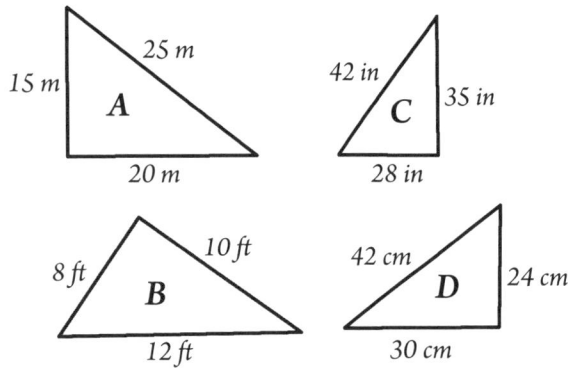

3) The ratio of boys to girls at Lark School
   is 6 to 5. $(B:G=6:5)$
a) Give the three thoughts associated
   with this ratio.

b) What proportion of the school is boys?

c) What proportion of the school is girls?

d) If there are 330 girls, then how many
   boys are there?

e) If there are 330 boys, then how many
   girls are there?

f) If there are 330 students at the school,
   then how many are girls and how many
   are boys?

4) Given that these two figures are similar,
   find X and Y.

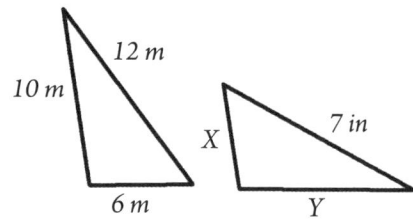

5) Give the four ways to express the ratio
   of this rectangle's dimensions.

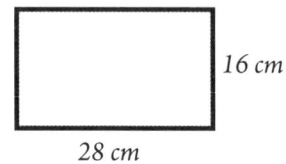

6) Convert each of these fractions into a
   decimal (perhaps repeating):
a) $5/9$

b) $5/11$

c) $5/16$

d) $5/27$

7) John is in the process of converting $^5/_{17}$ into a repeating decimal. At this moment, his work (which is completely correct, but not yet finished) looks like this:

```
          .2941176470588
    17 | 5.0000000000000
        -3 4
        ‾‾‾‾‾
         1 60
        -1 53
        ‾‾‾‾‾
            70
           -68
           ‾‾‾
            20
           -17
           ‾‾‾
            30
           -17
           ‾‾‾
           130
          -119
          ‾‾‾‾
           110
          -102
          ‾‾‾‾
            80
           -68
           ‾‾‾
           120
          -119
          ‾‾‾‾
            10
          -  0
          ‾‾‾‾
           100
           -85
           ‾‾‾
           150
          -136
          ‾‾‾‾
           140
          -136
          ‾‾‾‾
             4
```

a) Under what condition will John finally be finished?

b) Given that the divisor is 17, what is the most number of digits that could appear under the repeat bar, if it ends up repeating?

c) Finish the problem.

8) Give an example of a fraction (with whole numbers in the numerator and denominator) that, when converted into a decimal, won't ever repeat or end.

Mental arithmetic

9) $71^2 =$

10) $41^2 =$

11) $21^2 =$

12) $22 \times 18 =$

13) $34 \times 26 =$

14) $97 \times 103 =$

15) $53^2 =$

16) $24 \times 26 =$

Review

17) $7\frac{1}{2}$ m = _____ cm

18) 1.34 m = _____ mm

19) 60,000 mg = _____ kg

20) What is 300 decreased by 7%?

21) Do it in your head:
  a) 6 is what percent of 18?

  b) 40 is what percent of 80?

  c) 6000 is what percent of 8000?

  d) 8 is what percent of 48?

  e) 800 is what percent of 3200?

  f) 140 is what percent of 210?

22) $(0.02)^5$

23) $\sqrt{25,000,000}$

24) $\sqrt{8,100,000,000}$

25) $\sqrt[4]{8,100,000,000}$

26) $5\frac{1}{2} \times 2\frac{2}{3}$

27) $5\frac{1}{2} - 2\frac{2}{3}$

28) $2\frac{2}{3} \div 5\frac{1}{2}$

Ratios II – Sheet 2

1) What can be said about any two similar figures?

2) Find X, given that these figures are similar:

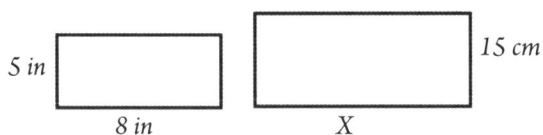

3) Find X and Y given that the two figures are similar:

4) Using a ruler with this rectangle.

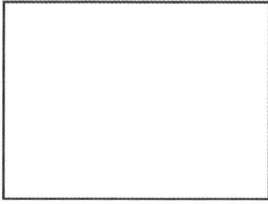

a) What is the length of its base in centimetres (to the nearest tenth of a cm)?

b) What is its height in centimetres?

c) Calculate the ratio of base to height in decimal form (to three significant digits).

d) Calculate the ratio of height to base in decimal form (to three significant digits).

5) Use the same rectangle as given with the previous problem.
a) What is the base's length in millimetres (to the nearest mm)?

b) What is its height in millimetres?

c) Calculate the ratio of base to height in decimal form (to three significant digits).

d) Calculate the ratio of height to base in decimal form (to three significant digits).

6) State the two laws of repeating decimals.

7) Bill weighs 60 kg and Jeff weighs 42 kg.
a) What is the ratio of their weights?

b) What is the ratio of the distances that they must sit from the fulcrum?

c) If Bill sits 2.1 m out from the fulcrum of a see-saw, then how far out does Jeff need to sit for the see-saw to balance?

d) If Jeff sits 3.2 m out from the fulcrum of a see-saw, then how far out does Bill need to sit for the see-saw to balance?

e) What does this statement mean? With a balanced seesaw, a person's weight, and the distance that he must sit from the fulcrum, are *inversely proportional.*

8) Sue averaged 60 km/h when driving to Betty's house on Monday, and the trip took her 30 minutes.

a) How far did Sue drive to get to Betty's house?

b) If Sue does the same trip on Tuesday, but drives at ⅘ of Monday's speed, then what would her average speed be, and how long would the trip take?

c) If Sue does the same trip on Wednesday, but drives at ³⁄₂ of Monday's speed, then what would her average speed be, and how long would the trip take?

d) What does the following statement mean?
When travelling, speed and time are *inversely proportional*.

Mental arithmetic

9) $31^2 =$

10) $61^2 =$

11) $91^2 =$

12) $56^2 =$

13) $35 \times 14 =$

14) $84 \times 76 =$

15) $280 \div 350 =$

16) $180 \times 500 =$

Review

17) Do it in your head:

a) What is 35 increased by 20%?

b) What is 35 decreased by 20%?

c) What is 35 increased by 80%?

d) What is 35 decreased by 80%?

18) $25\frac{5}{6} + 37\frac{1}{18}$

19) $\left(3\frac{4}{7}\right)^2$

20) $\dfrac{2\frac{5}{8}}{6\frac{3}{4}}$

Ratios II – Sheet 3

1) A triangle has a base equal to 3.7 cm and a height equal to 2.4 cm. Give the four ways to write the ratio of these dimensions. (Give your answers as exact, perhaps repeating, decimals.)

2) With each figure below give your best guess (don't measure) of what the ratio is of the two labelled dimensions. Give your answers in whole number form.

a)

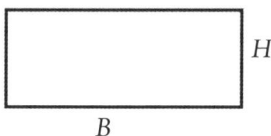

b)

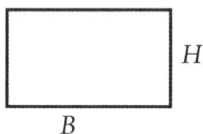

c) A square

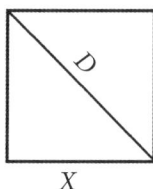

d) A circle

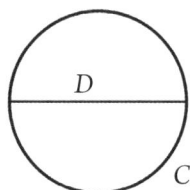

3) A rectangle's base is 22 cm and its height is 8 cm.
a) Give the ratio of base to height in decimal form.

b) Give the two thoughts associated with the above ratio.

4) The ratio of boys to girls in a school is 7 to 5. If there are 420 students, then how many are boys and how many are girls?

5) Find X given that the two rectangles are similar:

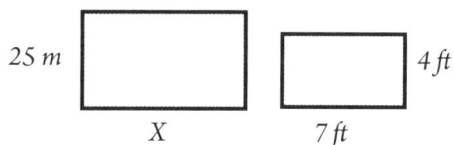

6) The ratio of Henry's money to Jeff's money is 7 to 4. How much does Henry have if Jeff has £25?

Mental arithmetic

7) $41 \times 16 =$

8) $49 \times 18 =$

9) $81 \times 12 =$

10) $102 \times 98 =$

11) $160 \times 55 =$

12) $6000 \div 120 =$

13) $315 \times 4 =$

14) $770 \times 11 =$

Review

15) 30 is 50% of what number?

16) 140 is 25% of what number?

17) 36 to 48 is what percentage increase?

18) 48 to 36 is what percentage decrease?

19) What is 50 decreased by 20% and then that result increased by 20%?

20) On Mike's bike trip, he always rode at a speed of 18 km/h. On the first day he rode for a total of 6 hours.

a) How far did he cycle on the first day?

b) If he rode for ⅔ as long on the second day, then how long did he ride for, and how far did he go?

c) Circle the correct answer. This means that if he rides for ⅔ as long, then he goes   ⅔ as far,
                  3⁄2 as far?

d) If he rode for 4⁄3 as long on the third day as on the first day, then how long did he ride for, and how far did he go?

e) Circle the correct answer. This means that if he rides for 4⁄3 as long, then he goes   4⁄3 as far,
                  ¾ as far?

f) What does the following statement mean?
   Time and distance are *directly proportional.*

21) Given that the strings on Mike's violin are 28.5 cm long, and that the A string has a frequency of 440 hz:

a) Mike plays the note E (which is the fifth above A) on the A string by pressing down at ⅔ of the string's length. How far from the end of the string (i.e. from the bridge) is he pressing down when playing this E note? (Give your answer in cm.)

b) What is the frequency of this E note?

c) The note C has a frequency of 550 hz. What is the ratio of the frequencies of note C to note A?

d) In order to play the note C on the A string, what is the ratio of the length of the whole string to the length of the vibrating portion of the string?

e) In order to play the note C on the A string, how far from the end of the string (i.e. from the bridge) must Mike press down?

f) What does the following statement mean?
With any string instrument, the length of the string, and the frequency (i.e. pitch) of the note, are *inversely proportional*.

The wonder of 7

22) Convert each fraction into a repeating decimal. Look for patterns:

a) $\frac{1}{7}$

b) $\frac{2}{7}$

c) $\frac{3}{7}$

d) $\frac{4}{7}$

e) $\frac{5}{7}$

f) $\frac{6}{7}$

23) Look for patterns:
a) $142{,}857 \times 1 =$

b) $142{,}857 \times 2 =$

c) $142{,}857 \times 3 =$

d) $142{,}857 \times 4 =$

e) $142{,}857 \times 5 =$

f) $142{,}857 \times 6 =$

g) $142{,}857 \times 7 =$

24) Add:
a) $14 + 28 + 57 =$

b) $142 + 857 =$

Ratios II – Sheet 4

1) Convert to a repeating decimal:
a) $9/13$

b) $13/9$

2) Bill weighs 75 kg and Jeff weighs 60 kg. If Bill sits 2.8 m out from the fulcrum of a seesaw, then how far out does Jeff need to sit for the seesaw to balance?

3) A cat weighs 6 kg and a dog weighs 16 kg. Give the four ways to express the ratio of these weights.

4) Cathy is training for a bike race. Each day she times how long it takes to go a distance of 4.3 km up a hill. On Monday it took her exactly 15 minutes. She calculated that her average speed was therefore 17.2 km/h. On Tuesday she covered that same distance in just $4/5$ of the time that it took on Monday. On Wednesday it took her $7/6$ as long as it

did on Monday (give your answer to three significant digits):
a) How long did it take her on Tuesday?

b) What was her average speed on Tuesday?

c) How long did it take her on Wednesday?

d) What was her average speed on Wednesday?

5) Jen is training for a bike race. Each day she sees how far she can cycle up a hill in 9 minutes. On Monday she went 1.92 km up the hill, and calculated that her average speed was 12.8 km/h. On Tuesday she was tired and only went $5/6$ as far as she did on Monday. But on Wednesday she went $9/8$ as far as she did on Monday. (Give your answer to three significant digits.)
a) How far did she cycle on Tuesday?

b) What was her average speed on Tuesday?

c) How far did she cycle on Wednesday?

d) What was her average speed on Wednesday?

6) With the triangle below:

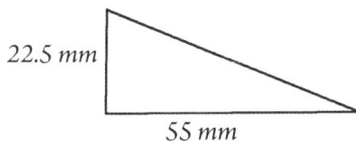

22.5 mm

55 mm

a) Give the ratio of base to height in whole number form.

b) Give the three thoughts associated with the above ratio.

c) Give the ratio of base to height in decimal form.

d) Give the two thoughts associated with the above ratio.

e) Give the ratio of height to base in decimal form.

f) Give the two thoughts associated with the above ratio.

A square's ratio

7) In the space below, carefully construct a square with a compass and straight-edge that has fairly long sides. Measure, as accurately as possible, the length of the side (X) and the length of the diagonal (D). Using long division, calculate the ratio of the diagonal to the side $(D:X)$, and also the ratio of the side to the diagonal $(X:D)$, both in decimal form. (Go to three significant figures with your division.)

a) $D:X \approx$

b) $X:D \approx$

Ratios II – Sheet 5

1) There are 12 boys and 16 girls:
a) Give the ratio of boys to girls in whole number form.

b) Give the three thoughts associated with the above ratio.

c) Give the ratio of boys to girls in decimal form.

d) Give the two thoughts associated with the above ratio.

2) A recipe calls for 1150 mℓ of water and 700 mℓ of flour.
a) What is the ratio of flour to water?

b) If the recipe needs to be enlarged, how much water is needed for 1ℓ of flour (to the nearest 10 mℓ)?

3) *The four ratios of a square*
a) Give the approximate ratio of the side (*X*) to the diagonal (*D*) of a square in whole number form, and write down the three thoughts associated with it.

b) Give the approximate ratio of the diagonal to the side of a square in whole number form, and write down the three thoughts associated with it.

c) Give the approximate ratio of the side to the diagonal of a square in decimal form, and write down the two thoughts associated with it.

d) Give the approximate ratio of the diagonal to the side of a square in decimal form, and write down the two thoughts associated with it.

4) Use one of the four ratios of a square (given above) to answer these questions.
a) What is the length of the diagonal of a square that has a side of length 15 m?

b) What is the length of the side of a square that has a diagonal of length 9 m?

5) Find X:

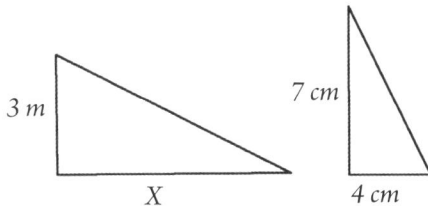

6) The ratio of men to women at Bill's college is 7 to 4.
a) If there are 658 men, then how many women are there?

b) If there are 1,600 women, then how many men are there?

A circle's ratio

7) Find a fairly large, nearly perfect circle (e.g. a bicycle wheel). Measure, as accurately as possible, the length of the circumference (C) and the length of the diameter (D). Using long division, calculate the ratio of the diameter to the circumference (D : C), and also the ratio of the circumference to the diameter (C : D), both in decimal form. (Go to three significant figures with your division.)

a) D : C ≈

b) C : D ≈

Ratios II – Sheet 6

1) Use one of the four ratios of a square (see previous sheet) to answer these questions. (The easiest method will vary from problem to problem.)
a) What is the length of the diagonal of a square that has a 35 cm side?

b) What is the length of the side of a square that has a 21 m diagonal?

c) What is the length of the diagonal of a square that has a 3 mm side?

d) What is the length of the side of a square that has a 2 m diagonal?

2) *The four ratios of a circle*
a) Give the approximate ratio of the circumference to the diameter of a circle in whole number form, and write down the three thoughts associated with it.

b) Give the approximate ratio of the diameter to the circumference of a circle in whole number form, and write down the three thoughts associated with it.

c) Give the approximate ratio of the circumference to the diameter of a circle in decimal form, and write down the two thoughts associated with it.

d) Give the approximate ratio of the diameter to the circumference of a circle in decimal form, and write down the two thoughts associated with it.

3) Use one of the four ratios of a circle (given above) to answer these questions.
a) Find the circumference of a circle that has a 21 m diameter.

b) Find the diameter of a circle that has a 330 cm circumference.

4) Pretend, for this problem, that you never saw the decimal values for the ratios of a circle as just given.
In order to calculate the ratio of the circumference to the diameter of a circle (see previous worksheet), Joe measured the diameter and circumference of a jar and got 4.4 cm and 14.4 cm, respectively. Using Joe's measurements, calculate the ratio of the length of the diameter to the circumference, and also the ratio of the length

of the circumference to the diameter, both in decimal form. (Round your answer to three significant figures.)

$D : C =$

$C : D =$

Mental arithmetic

5) $31 \times 15 =$

6) $39 \times 120 =$

7) $49 \times 15 =$

8) $22 \div 4 =$

9) $834 - 795 =$

10) $31^2 =$

11) $52^2 =$

12) $43 \times 37 =$

Review

13) $0.07 \, \ell =$ _____ mℓ

14) $7 \, mg =$ _____ g

15) $0.08 \, mm =$ _____ m

16) 72 is 66⅔% of what number?

17) 580 is 22% of what number?

18) Going from 200 down to 180 is what percentage decrease?

19) Going from 180 up to 200 is what percentage increase?

20) Convert to a fraction:
   a) 33⅓%

   b) 37.5%

   c) 85%

21) Convert to a mixed number: $\frac{64}{7}$

22) Convert to an improper fraction: $8\frac{4}{5}$

23) What is $68\frac{2}{15} - \frac{5}{6}$?

Ratios II – Sheet 7

1) The ratio of Ron's weight to Tom's weight is 6 to 5 ($R:T = 6:5$).

a) What are the three thoughts (as equations only) associated with this ratio?

b) What is Tom's weight if Ron weighs 57 kg?

c) What is Ron's weight if Tom weighs 45 kg?

2) Find X and Y, given that the two triangles are similar.

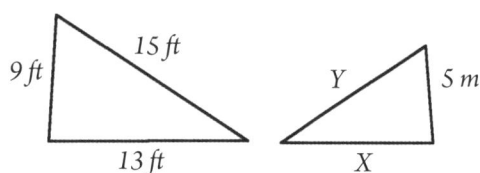

3) In your own words, explain what π is.

4) In your own words, explain what a *rational number* is.

5) In your own words, explain what an *irrational number* is.

6) *Calculating decimal values*

a) To calculate the decimal value of $^{31}/_{55}$ Jeff does $31 \div 55$ on his calculator, which shows up as 0.56363636364. Is this answer exact?

b) What is the exact value of $^{31}/_{55}$ as a decimal?

c) Jeff calculates $\sqrt{30}$ on his calculator, which shows up as 5.47722557505. Is this answer exact?

d) What is the exact value of $\sqrt{30}$ as a decimal?

7) a) Calculate $^{22}/_7$ as a repeating decimal.

b) Is $^{22}/_7$ larger than, or smaller than, the actual value for π?

8) *The ratio in a circle*
  a) What are the three thoughts associated with the ratio $C : D \approx 22 : 7$

  b) What are the three thoughts associated with the ratio $D : C \approx 7 : 22$

  c) What are the two thoughts associated with the ratio $C : D \approx 3.14 : 1$

  d) What are the two thoughts associated with the ratio $D : C \approx 0.318 : 1$

  e) Find the diameter of a circle that has a 77 m circumference.

  f) Find the circumference of a circle that has an 8 cm diameter.

g) Find the circumference of a circle that has a 77 m diameter.

h) Find the diameter of a circle that has a 4 cm circumference.

9) *The ratio in a square*
  a) What are the three thoughts associated with the ratio $D : X \approx 7 : 5$

  b) What are the three thoughts associated with the ratio $X : D \approx 5 : 7$

  c) What are the two thoughts associated with the ratio $D : X \approx 1.414 : 1$

  d) What are the two thoughts associated with the ratio $X : D \approx 0.707 : 1$

  e) Find the length of the diagonal of a square that has a 20 m side.

f) Find the length of the side of a square that has a 30 m diagonal.

g) Find the length of the diagonal of a square that has a 55 m side.

h) Find the length of the side of a square that has a 42 m diagonal.

Mental arithmetic

10) Multiply:

a)
$$\begin{array}{r} 32 \\ \times 23 \\ \hline \end{array}$$

b)
$$\begin{array}{r} 65 \\ \times 26 \\ \hline \end{array}$$

c)
$$\begin{array}{r} 45 \\ \times 83 \\ \hline \end{array}$$

11) $58^2 =$

12) $48 \times 52 =$

13) $61 \times 59 =$

14) $36 \div 99 =$

15) $7 \times 999 =$

Review

16) *Short Division.* Leave the answer as an exact decimal (perhaps repeating).
$903.5 \div 8000$

17) $5\frac{3}{5} \div 4$

18) $5\frac{3}{5} \times 4$

Ratios II – Sheet 8

1) With the triangle below:

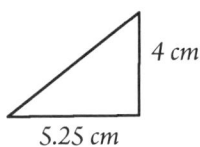

4 cm

5.25 cm

a) Give the ratio of base to height in whole number form.

b) Give the three thoughts associated with the above ratio.

2) A rectangle's base is 2¾ cm and its height is 1½ cm.
a) Give the ratio of base to height in decimal form.

b) Give the two thoughts associated with the above ratio.

3) Baby Jay weighs 3.5 kg and Baby Kay weighs 5.6 kg. Give the four ways to write the ratio of these weights.

Mental arithmetic
4) Multiply:
a) $\begin{array}{r} 42 \\ \times 35 \\ \hline \end{array}$

b) $\begin{array}{r} 75 \\ \times 84 \\ \hline \end{array}$

c) $\begin{array}{r} 47 \\ \times 69 \\ \hline \end{array}$

5) $49 \div 63 =$

6) $0.034 \times 10000 =$

7) $76 \times 11 =$

8) $41^2 =$

9) $51 \times 700 =$

Review
10) $18 \text{ m}\ell =$ _____ ℓ

11) $21 \text{ m} =$ _____ cm

12) ¾ m = _____ km

13) Think fractions!

a) 7 is what percent of 35?

b) 12 is what percent of 30?

c) 12 is what percent of 32?

14) A bike normally listed for £380 is on sale for a 35% discount. What is the new discounted price?

15) How much do you have to pay for the above bike, if you take an extended warranty for 7% of the price?

The ratio in a circle

16) a) Give each of the four ratios in a circle. For each ratio, state the one thought associated with it that you consider the most important.

b) Find the circumference of a circle that has a 35 m diameter.

c) Find the circumference of a circle that has a 3 m diameter.

d) Find the diameter of a circle that has a circumference of 44 m.

e) Find the diameter of a circle that has a circumference of 20 m.

The ratio in a square

17) a) Give each of the four ratios in a square. For each ratio, state the thought associated with it that you consider the most important.

b) Find the length of the side of a square that has a 35 m diagonal.

c) Find the length of the diagonal of a square that has a 60 cm side.

d) Find the length of the diagonal of a square that has a 35 m side.

e) Find the length of the side of a square that has a 4 m diagonal.

Pay rate, speed, etc. – Sheet 1

1) A train travels 450 km in 6 hours. What is its average speed?

2) Bill takes 5 hours to drive 330 km. What is his average speed?

3) Jean takes 3 hours and 45 minutes to drive 360 km. What is her average speed?

4) How much money does Kevin earn in two weeks, if he works 36 hours per week at £8.50/hr?

5) How long does it take Mary to cycle 72 km at 18 km/h?

6) How long does it take a plane to fly 2,900 km at 870 km/h?

7) What is Kate's hourly wage if she earns €345.60 for 32 hours of work?

8) Sophia works 4 hours per day, 6 days per week. If she earns £204 per week, then what is her hourly wage?

9) How much does Morgan earn if he baby-sits from 6:15 pm to 9:45 pm and charges £3.50/hr?

10) *Comparing speed*
   a) Ken is travelling at 50 mph. What does this mean?

   b) Henry is travelling at 60 km/h. What does this mean?

   c) Wilbur is travelling at 30 m/s. What does this mean?

   d) Making a good guess, and without doing any calculations, rank Ken, Henry and Wilbur from fastest to slowest.

Mental arithmetic

11) Multiply:

a)
$$\begin{array}{r} 85 \\ \times 61 \\ \hline \end{array}$$

b)
$$\begin{array}{r} 73 \\ \times 43 \\ \hline \end{array}$$

12) $15 \times 41 =$

13) $35 \times 45 =$

14) $2345 \div 9999 =$

15) $105 \times 106 =$

16) $180 \div 4 =$

17) $813 - 297 =$

Review

18) $42 \, \text{mm} = $ _____ m

19) $0.82 \, \text{g} = $ _____ mg

20) $12 \, \text{kg} = $ _____ g

21) $45 \, \text{mm} = $ _____ cm

22) $8 \, \text{mg} = $ _____ g

23) $3.9 \, \ell = $ _____ mℓ

24) Write the four ways to express the ratio of this rectangle's dimensions.

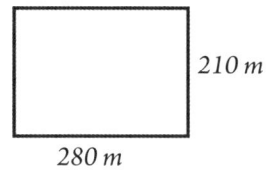

210 m

280 m

25) 240 up to 300 is what percentage increase?

26) 300 down to 240 is what percentage decrease?

27) Calculate $\sqrt{3844}$
(Hint: the answer is a whole number.)

Pay rate, speed, etc. – Sheet 2

1) Bill earns £7.75/hr.
a) What does he earn in a week, if he works 25 hours per week?

b) How long does he have to work in order to earn £434?

2) What is Beth's hourly pay if she earns £336 in a 35-hour workweek?

3) Mark earns €8.25/hr at Cathy's Café and €9.60/hr at a bank. How much does he earn in a week if he works 12 hours at the café and 22 hours at the bank?

4) How long does it take Bob to bike 105 km at 21 km/h?

5) John biked 18¾ km in 45 minutes. What was his average speed?

6) How many minutes does it take to skate 5¼ km at 18 km/h?

7) What is Mike's average speed if he bikes 43 km in 5 hours?

8) What is the fuel efficiency (in mpg – miles per gallon) of Mark's moped if it uses 1.4 gallons in 200 miles?

9) How far does a bus travel in 5 hours at a rate of 72 km/h?

10) How far does Kelsey run in 20 minutes at a rate of 3.2 m/s?

11) How far does Peter walk in 1½ hours at a rate of 5⅔ km/h?

12) Dan left his house at 12:55 to drive to Tom's house, 272 km away. If he drove at an average speed of 85 km/h, at what time did he arrive at Tom's house?

13) *Challenge*
Bill lives in Denver. He made 12 return trips to Boulder and 9 return trips to Colorado Springs, each time on the bus. The bus's average speed was always 50 mph, and the distance from Denver to Colorado Springs is 70 miles, and Denver to Boulder is 28 miles. What was the total amount of time Bill spent riding buses?

Mental arithmetic

14) Multiply:
a) $\begin{array}{r} 34 \\ \times 56 \\ \hline \end{array}$

b) $\begin{array}{r} 58 \\ \times 98 \\ \hline \end{array}$

15) $12 \times 61 =$

16) $61^2 =$

17) $23 \times 9999 =$

18) $2700 \div 3600 =$

19) $32 \times 5 =$

20) $9300 \div 5 =$

Review

21) The ratio in a square.
a) Give each of the four ratios in a square.

b) Find the length of the side of a square that has a 56 m diagonal.

c) Find the length of the diagonal of a square that has a 4 m side.

d) Find the length of the diagonal of a square that has a 85 cm side.

e) Find the length of the side of a square that has a 6 m diagonal.

Pay rate, speed, etc. – Sheet 3

1) How long does it take a train to travel 238 km at 85 km/h?

2) How far do you cycle in 3 hours and 40 minutes at 24 km/h?

3) Frank went 44 km in 3 hours in his boat. What was his average speed?

4) How long does it take a plane to fly 720 km at 900 km/h?

5) Vicky's car gets 42 mpg (miles/gal) on the motorway. How far can she drive on 11 gallons of petrol?

6) Beverly earned £1,440 last month in a total of 128 hours. What is her hourly wage?

7) Mary rows a boat at an average of 3 km/h. If it takes her 45 minutes to cross a lake, then how wide is the lake?

8) Karen works 40 hours per week at £15/hr. What is her annual salary? (Assume that she took two weeks unpaid holiday in the year.)

9) Martha started her bike trip by going up a 10-km hill in 2 hours, then going down a 6-km hill in 10 minutes. She then finished by biking along a 22 ½ km flat stretch in one hour and 20 minutes. What was her average speed:
a) Going up the hill?

b) Going down the hill?

c) Going on the flats?

d) For the whole trip?

10) Jean went 40 km in the first hour, 30 km in the second hour and 50 km in the third hour. What was the average speed for the trip?

11) A train went 80 km in the first hour, and then 176 km in the second hour. What was the average speed for the trip?

12) A train went 80 km in the first hour, and then went 176 km/h for the second, third and fourth hours. What was the average speed for the trip?

13) A train went 80 km in the first hour, and then went 528 km over the next three hours. What was the average speed for the trip?

14) What is your average speed (in mph) if you run a mile in 4 minutes?

Mental arithmetic

15) Multiply:
$$\begin{array}{r} 62 \\ \times 57 \\ \hline \end{array}$$

16) $13 \times 29 =$

17) $0.022 \div 4 =$

18) $0.63 \times 10 =$

19) $15 \times 440 =$

20) $109 \times 112 =$

21) $315 \div 35 =$

22) $103 \times 104 =$

The ratio in a circle

23) a) Give each of the four ratios in a circle.

b) Find the circumference of a circle that has a diameter of 28 m.

c) Find the circumference of a circle that has a diameter of 8.3 m.

d) Find the diameter of a circle that has a circumference of 44 cm.

e) Find the diameter of a circle with a circumference of 5 cm.

Pay rate, speed, etc. – Sheet 4

1) How long does it take to cycle 102 km at 18 km/h?

2) At 28 km/h, how far does someone travel:
a) In 10 hours?

b) In 5½ hours?

c) In 2 hours and 24 minutes?

3) Doris leaves her house at 8:25 to cycle to Tina's house, which is 40.5 km away. At what time does she arrive if she cycles at a rate of 18 km/h?

4) Bill travelled 24 km to Jeff's house at 6 km/h and then did the return trip at 24 km/h. What was the average speed for the trip?

5) Pete's car has a 12-gallon petrol tank and gets 34 mpg.
a) How much petrol does Pete need to drive 400 miles?

b) Pete is going to drive from New York City to San Francisco, which is about 2,900 miles. What is the least number of times that he will need to stop and refill his tank during the trip? (Assume that he starts with a full tank.)

6) Matt went 36 km in the first hour, 47 km in the second hour and 45 km in the third hour. What was his average speed for the trip?

7) *Challenge*
   Janet leaves home at 10:15 am, jogging at 12 km/h. At what time, and how far from home, will Sue catch her, if she leaves the same house at 10:35 am biking at 27 km/h?

8) Sally jogged at 6 km/h for 4 hours, and then biked at an average rate of 24 km/h for an hour. What was the average speed for the five hours?

9) The previous problem is the same as what other problem on this sheet?

10) Alice biked up a gradual 20-km uphill road at 5 km/h, and then came down at 15 km/h. What was her average speed for the whole trip?

11) Kelly is training for a running race. She is trying to improve how far she can run in one hour. (Circle the correct answers.)
   a) If she increases her average speed, then the distance that she runs in one hour will *increase / decrease?*

   b) Therefore, we can say that speed and distance are *directly / inversely proportional?*

   c) If she ran $\frac{7}{8}$ as fast today as she did yesterday, then in one hour today she went $\frac{7}{8}$ *as far /* $\frac{8}{7}$ *as far* as yesterday?

12) Jake is biking to Pete's house. (Circle the correct answers.)
   a) If Jake increases his speed, then his time for the trip *increases / decreases?*

   b) Therefore, we can say that speed and time are *directly / inversely proportional?*

   c) If he biked $\frac{7}{8}$ as fast today as he did yesterday, then the time it takes Jake to get to Pete's house today is $\frac{7}{8}$ *as long /* $\frac{8}{7}$ *as long* as yesterday?

13) Frank is travelling on a train that is going a steady speed. (Circle the correct answers.)
   a) If he increases the amount of time that he stays on the train, then will the distance he travels *increase / decrease?*

   b) Therefore, we can say that distance and time are *directly / inversely proportional?*

   c) If Frank sat on the train today for $\frac{7}{8}$ as long as yesterday, then today he went $\frac{7}{8}$ *as far /* $\frac{8}{7}$ *as far* as yesterday?

Mental arithmetic
14) Multiply:
$$\begin{array}{r} 46 \\ \times 35 \\ \hline \end{array}$$

15) $8 \times 59 =$

16) $25 \times 31 =$

17) $260 \times 15 =$

18) $240 \div 25 =$

90

19) $12 \times 39 =$

20) $140 \div 5 =$

21) 15% of £46 =

Review

22) What is 83⅓% of 420?

23) What is 160% of 55?

24) 8 is what percent of 40?

25) 32 is what percent of 40?

26) 9 is 6% of what number?

27) 12 is 66⅔% of what number?

Pay rate, speed, etc. – Sheet 5

1) How far do you walk in 4 hours and 15 minutes at a rate of 3.75 km/h?

2) Denise works an average of 7 hours per day and 22 days per month at an hourly wage of £24/hr.
a) How much does she earn in a month?

b) How long does it take her to earn £200?

c) How long does it take her to earn £10,000?

3) Jake works 40 hours per week and 40 weeks per year, and has a salary of £19,000/year. What does he earn per hour?

4) Crystal bikes 30 km to Kate's house in just one hour. On the way back home it takes her 2½ hours. What is her average speed:
a) Getting to Kate's house?

b) Returning home?

c) For the whole trip?

Average speed

5) For each problem, don't calculate a value; simply indicate whether the average speed is less than, equal to or greater than 12 km/h.

a) Bob ran 15 km in the first hour, and then 9 km in the second hour.

b) Benny ran from home to the river at 15 km/h and then ran back at 9 km/h.

6) What does it mean to say that:

a) Speed and time are *inversely proportional?*

b) Speed and distance are *directly proportional?*

7) Sam drove 450 km in 5 hours yesterday, which is an average of 90 km/h.

a) If he drives the same speed today, then how far will he travel if he drives for $\frac{5}{6}$ as much time?

b) If he drives the same speed today, then how far will he travel if he drives for $\frac{6}{5}$ as much time?

c) If he drives $\frac{5}{6}$ as fast today, then how long will it take him to travel 450 km?

d) If he drives $\frac{6}{5}$ as fast today, then how long will it take him to travel 450 km?

8) Bill measured that he went 420 km on the highway in 4 hours and 15 minutes, and used 23.5 litres of petrol. Round each answer to three significant digits.

a) What was his average speed?

b) If he had gone the same distance at $\frac{3}{4}$ the speed, then how long would it have taken him?

c) If he had driven at the same speed (as found in part a), but for $\frac{3}{4}$ the amount of time, then how far would he have gone?

d) What was the fuel efficiency (in ℓ/100 km) of his car for his original trip?

e) Around town, his car gets $\frac{2}{3}$ the fuel efficiency as on the motorway. How much petrol would be needed to drive the same distance (420 km) in town?

9) Jill went from her house to Mary's house (72 km away) at 45 km/h, and then returned at twice that speed. What was her average speed for going round trip?

10) *Challenge*
A train leaves London at 112 km/h toward Aberdeen (872 km away) at 1:20. At 1:50, another train leaves Aberdeen, heading for London, at 80 km/h. At what time, and how far from London, do they pass one another?

Mental arithmetic

11) $70 \times 890 =$

12) $81^2 =$

13) $135 \div 45 =$

14) $12 \times 999 =$

15) $3200 \div 2400 =$

16) $107^2 =$

17) $220 \times 45 =$

18) $2027 - 1989 =$

Review

19) $128\ m\ell =$ _____ ℓ

20) $4\frac{1}{4}\ km =$ _____ m

21) How much do you have to pay by mail order for a jacket marked at €280 if there is a 4.3% delivery charge?

22) Lenny paid £319.50 for a delivered bike marked at £300.00. What percent was the delivery charge?

Pay rate, speed, etc. – Sheet 6

1) A small plane flies 1,400 km in 4 hours and 10 minutes.
a) What is the average speed for the flight?

b) At that rate of speed, how far does the plane fly in 5 hours and 45 minutes?

c) At that rate of speed, how long does it take for the plane to fly 2,520 km?

2) A car uses 9.5 ℓ of petrol in 140 km.
a) What is its fuel efficiency (in ℓ/100 km, to 3 significant figures) for the trip?

b) Given the above fuel efficiency, how far can the car go on 48 ℓ of petrol?

3) Gordon biked 108 km in 4 hours yesterday, which is an average speed of 27 km/h.
a) If he bikes ⁸⁄₉ as fast today, then how long will it take him to cycle the 108 km?

b) If he bikes ⁹⁄₈ as fast today, then how long will it take him to cycle the 108 km?

c) If he bikes ⁸⁄₉ as fast today, then how far will he cycle in 4 hours?

d) If he bikes ⁹⁄₈ as fast today, then how far will he cycle in 4 hours?

4) Water is leaking out of a tank at a rate of 20 mℓ every minute. How long does it take 6 ℓ to leak out of the tank?

5) Benny biked up a 5-km long hill in 30 minutes, and then came back down the same route in 6 minutes. What was his average speed:
a) Going up the hill?

b) Going down the hill?

c) Round trip?

6) Sue biked 9 km to the beach at 30 km/h and returned (along the same route) at a rate of 18 km/h. What was her average speed for the whole trip?

London at a rate of 800 km/h. At what time, and how far from London, do they pass?

7) In 2003 Tim Montgomery broke the world record by running the 100 m sprint in 9.87 seconds.
a) What was his average speed for the race in m/s?

9) *Challenge*
A car thief crosses a bridge at 9:37 going 96 km/h in a car. At 9:49 a police car chasing the thief and going 120 km/h crosses the same bridge. Assuming that the cars maintain their speeds, at what time, and how far from the bridge, does the police car catch the thief?

b) *Challenge*
Calculate his average speed in km/h.

c) *Challenge*
Calculate his average speed in miles per hour (use 1 km ≈ 0.62 mi)

Mental arithmetic
10) Multiply:
$$\begin{array}{r} 26 \\ \times\, 33 \\ \hline \end{array}$$

11) $216 - 197 =$

12) $332 \div 5 =$

13) $155 \times 4 =$

14) $260 \times 11 =$

8) *Challenge*
A plane leaves London at 2:10 (GMT) and flies at a rate of 900 km/h toward Athens, 2,400 km away. At 2:30 (GMT), another plane leaves Athens toward

15) $63 \times 67 =$

16) $296.5 \div 100 =$

17) $35 \times 11 =$

Review

18) Find *X* and *Y* given that the two triangles are similar.

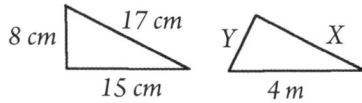
8 cm   17 cm   Y   X   15 cm   4 m

19) What is 4,800 decreased by 62½%?

20) What is 42 increased by 350%?

Geometry – Sheet 1

1) a) Find *X*.

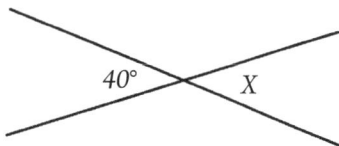
40°   X

b) The two labelled angles above are _____ angles.

2) a) Find *X*.

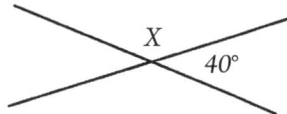
X   40°

b) The two labelled angles above are _____ angles.

3) Find *X*.

a)

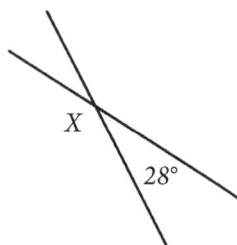
X   28°

b)

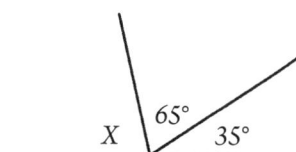
65°   X   35°

4) Find *X*.

a)

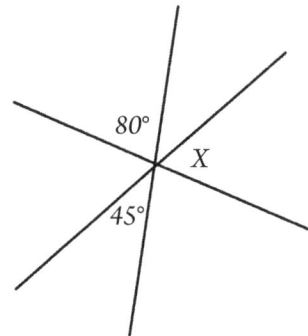
80°   X   45°

b)

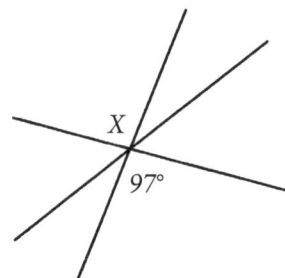
X   97°

c)

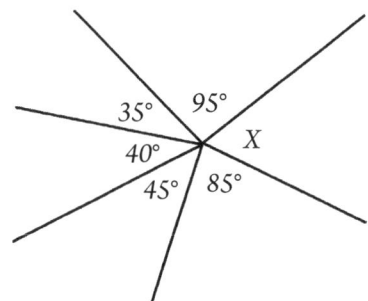
35°   95°   40°   X   45°   85°

5) Find the area of each square.

a)

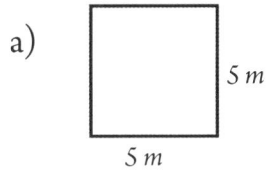

5 m

5 m

b)

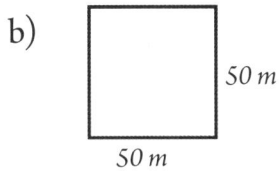

50 m

50 m

c)

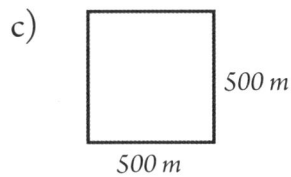

500 m

500 m

6) Find the area and perimeter.

a)

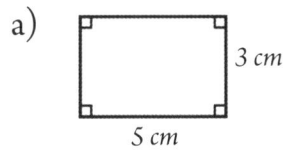

3 cm

5 cm

b)

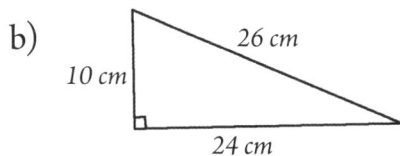

26 cm

10 cm

24 cm

c)

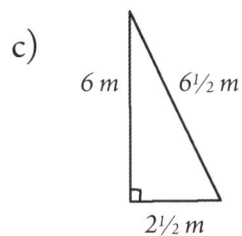

6 m   6½ m

2½ m

Mental arithmetic

7) Multiply

63
×95

8) $36 \times 5 =$

9) $48{,}000 \times 25 =$

10) $947 \div 999 =$

11) $51^2 =$

12) $35 \times 22 =$

13) $800 \div 25 =$

14) $21^2 =$

Review

15) 0.0003 kg = _____ g

16) 60 mm = _____ m

17) 0.562 m = _____ cm

18) Write the four ways to express the ratio of this rectangle's dimensions.

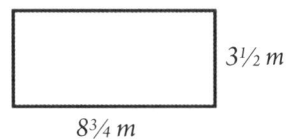

3½ m

8¾ m

The ratio in a circle

19) a) Give each of the four ratios in a circle.

b) Find the circumference of a circle that has a diameter of 5 m.

c) Find the circumference of a circle that has a diameter of 14 cm.

d) Find the diameter of a circle that has a circumference of 14 cm.

e) Find the diameter of a circle that has a circumference of 220 cm.

The ratio in a square

20) a) Give each of the four ratios in a square.

b) Find the length of the diagonal of a square that has a 45 m side.

c) Find the length of the diagonal of a square that has a 32 m side.

d) Find the length of the side of a square that has a 77 cm diagonal.

e) Find the length of the side of a square that has a 32 cm diagonal.

Geometry – Sheet 2

On all of the sheets in this unit, assume that lines are parallel if they appear to be so.

1) a) Find *X*.

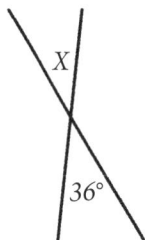

36°

b) The two labelled angles are _____ angles.

2) a) Find *X*.

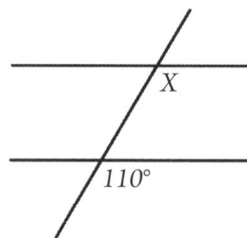

X

110°

b) The two labelled angles above are _____ angles.

3) a) Find X.

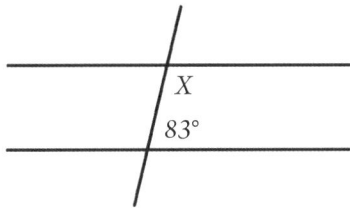

b) The two labelled angles above are
   _____ angles.

4) a) Find X.

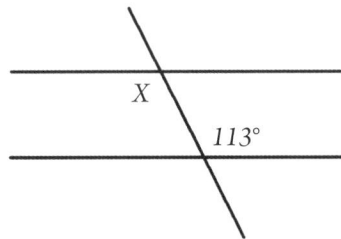

b) The two labelled angles above are
   _____ angles.

5) Find each variable.

a)

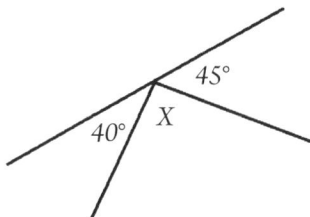

b)

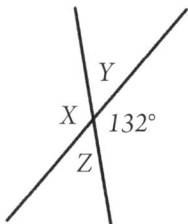

c)

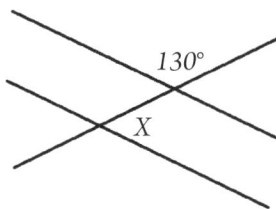

d)

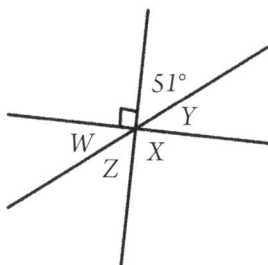

6) Give the dimensions of three different
   triangles that each have an area equal to
   24 square metres.

7) Find the area and perimeter.

a)

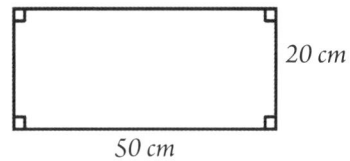

20 cm

50 cm

b)

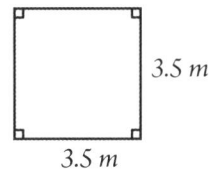

3.5 m

3.5 m

c)

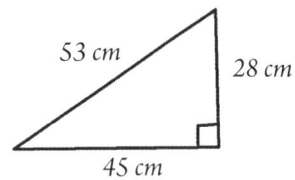

53 cm

28 cm

45 cm

d)

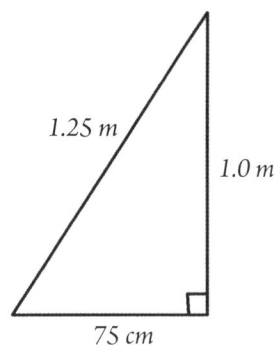

1.25 m

1.0 m

75 cm

8) Find the area of both the rectangle and the parallelogram.

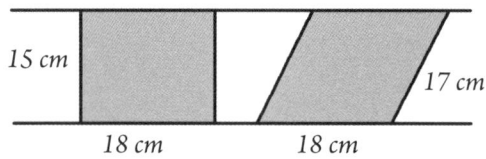

9) Find the area of the three triangles, below, given that the middle one is a right triangle.

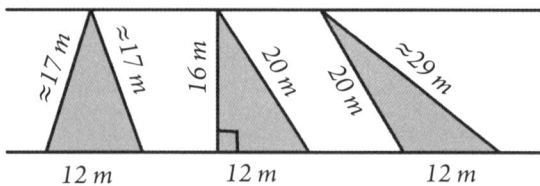

10) Explain the Pythagorean Theorem to an adult.
Notes for the adult: The formula $c^2 = a^2 + b^2$ is not used until Class 8. Please comment on the student's explanation in the space below.

Mental arithmetic

11) Multiply:

$$\begin{array}{r} 85 \\ \times 24 \\ \hline \end{array}$$

12) $53 \times 47 =$

13) $36 \times 25 =$

14) $45 \times 18 =$

15) $68 \times 72 =$

16) $320 \times 5 =$

17) $56{,}000 \div 800 =$

18) $54^2 =$

Review

19) Find X given that the two rectangles are similar.

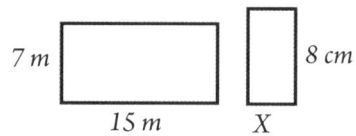

20) At a rate of 18 km/h, how far do you cycle in 2 hours and 45 minutes?

21) Hairy Kennel has 140 dogs and 220 cats:

a) Give the ratio of dogs to cats in whole number form.

b) Give the three thoughts associated with the above ratio.

c) Give the ratio of dogs to cats in decimal form.

d) Give the two thoughts associated with the above ratio.

e) The other kennel in town has the same ratio of dogs to cats. If that kennel has 126 dogs and cats combined, then how many are dogs and how many are cats?

Geometry – Sheet 3

1) Find the area.

a)

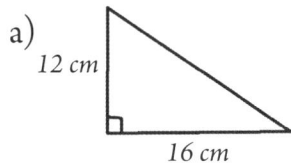
12 cm
16 cm

b)

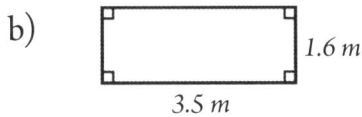
1.6 m
3.5 m

c)

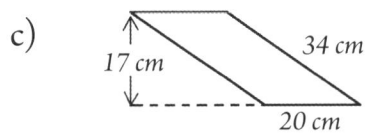
17 cm
34 cm
20 cm

d)

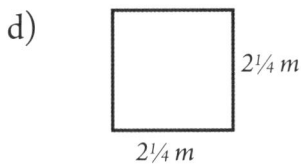
2¼ m
2¼ m

e)

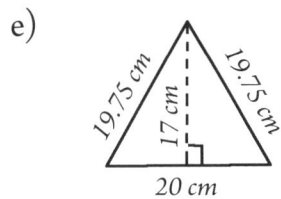
19.75 cm
17 cm
19.75 cm
20 cm

2) Use this drawing to answer the following questions.

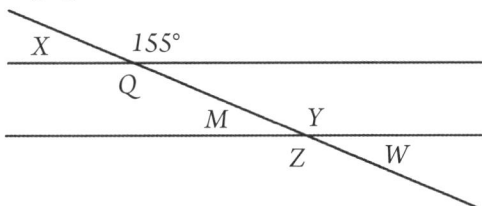
X   155°
Q
M   Y
Z   W

a) Find each variable.

b) Z and W are _____ angles.

c) Z and Y are _____ angles.

d) Z and Q are _____ angles.

e) Q and M are _____ angles.

f) Q and Y are _____ angles.

g) X and M are _____ angles.

3) Find the area and perimeter of:

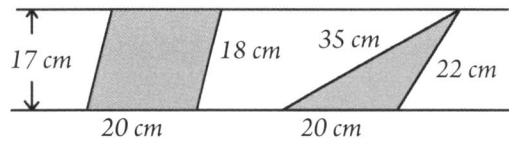
17 cm   18 cm   35 cm
22 cm
20 cm   20 cm

a) The parallelogram.

b) The triangle.

4) Find each variable.

a)

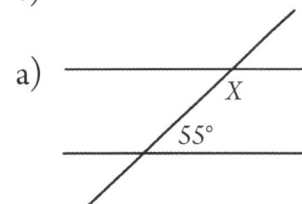
X
55°

b)

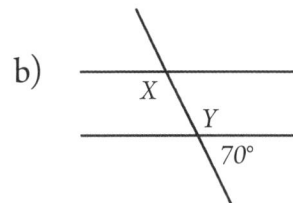
X
Y
70°

c)

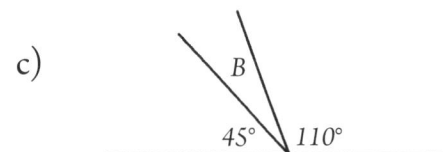
B
45° 110°

5) *ABCD* is a square with 16 cm sides. $\overline{AE}$ and $\overline{FC}$ both equal 4 cm.

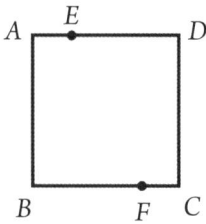

a) Find the area of the square *ABCD*.

b) Find the area of the triangle *ABC*.

c) Find the area of the triangle *EBC*.

d) Find the area of the triangle *ABF*.

e) Find the area of the triangle *EBF*.

f) Find the area of the triangle *DBF*.

g) Find the area of the trapezium *ABCE*.

h) Find the area of the trapezium *ABFE*.

i) Find the length of line segment *AF*.

6) On a separate sheet, use a compass, straightedge and protractor to construct a triangle having angles *A*, *B* and *C*, such that it has the given angle measurements. Then, calculate the degree measures of the missing angle(s). Lastly, check your calculations by measuring those missing angles with a protractor.

a) $\angle A = 90°$ and $\angle B = 65°$
$\angle C =$

b) $\angle A = 15°$ and $\angle B = 20°$
$\angle C =$

c) All angles are equal.
$\angle A = \angle B = \angle C =$

d) An isosceles triangle where the angle contained by the two equal sides is 100°.
$\angle A = 100°$
$\angle B =$
$\angle C =$

Mental arithmetic

7) $93 \times 97 =$

8) $5.2 \div 10,000 =$

9) $59 \times 11 =$

10) $52^2 =$

11) $7 \times 9999 =$

12) $3.2 \div 4 =$

13) $1800 \div 3000 =$

14) $6400 \div 4 =$

Review

15) 0.007 kg = _____ mg

16) 72 ℓ = _____ mℓ

17) A train went 80 km in the first hour, and then went 210 km over the next three hours. What was the average speed over the four hours?

18) A car used 2.3 gallons of petrol in 60 miles. What was its fuel efficiency (in mpg) for the trip?

19) What is 4,000 increased by 63%?

Geometry – Sheet 4

1) Find the area and perimeter.

a)

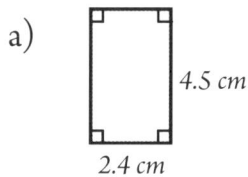

4.5 cm

2.4 cm

b)

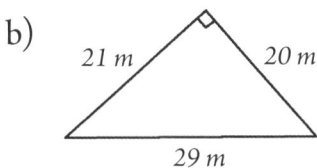

21 m   20 m

29 m

2) Find each variable.

a)

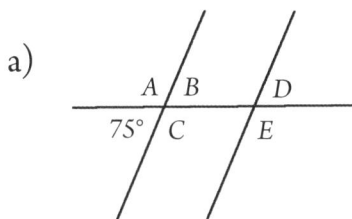

A / B   D

75° / C   E

b)

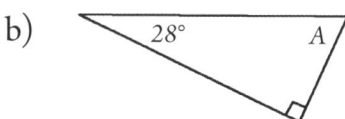

28°   A

3) Using Pythagoras's formula to find Pythagorean triples.

A Pythagorean triple is a special right triangle where all three sides (X, Y and Z) have lengths that are whole numbers. Pythagoras's formula is:

$$X = 2n + 1$$
$$Y = 2n^2 + 2n$$
$$Z = 2n^2 + 2n + 1$$

The table below shows different Pythagorean triples by choosing different values for n. Fill in the table by using the formulas given above.

n	X	Y	Z
1			
2			
3			
4			
5			
6			

4) Using the Arabian formula to find Pythagorean triples.
The Arabian formula is (where $u > v$):

$$X = u^2 - v^2$$
$$Y = 2uv$$
$$Z = u^2 + v^2$$

The table below shows different Pythagorean triples by choosing different values for u and v. Fill in the table by using the formulas given above.

u	v	X	Y	Z
2	1			
4	1			
6	1			
8	1			
3	2			

u	v	X	Y	Z
5	2			
7	2			
9	2			
4	3			
8	3			
5	4			
7	4			
9	4			
6	5			
8	5			
7	6			

Geometry – Sheet 5

1) Find the area.

a)

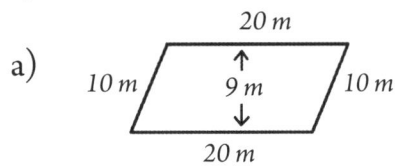

20 m
10 m   9 m   10 m
20 m

b)

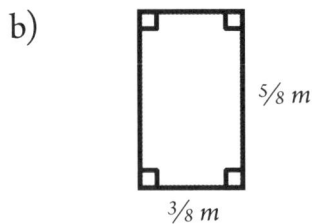

$5/8$ m
$3/8$ m

c)

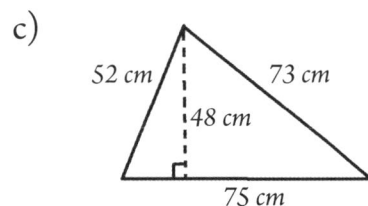

52 cm   73 cm
48 cm
75 cm

d)

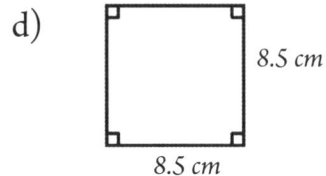

8.5 cm
8.5 cm

e)

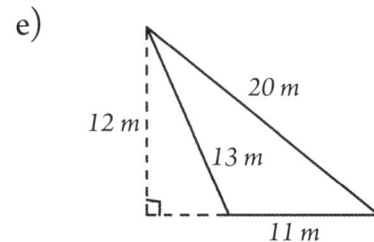

20 m
12 m   13 m
11 m

2) Find the variables.

a)

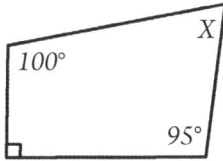

b) *Challenge*

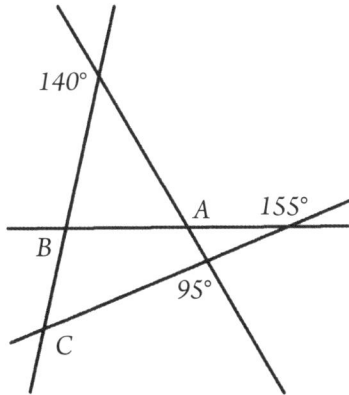

c)

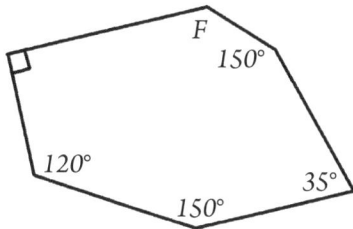

3) What is the measure of the interior angles of a regular hexagon?

4) Calculate the value for *X*.

a)

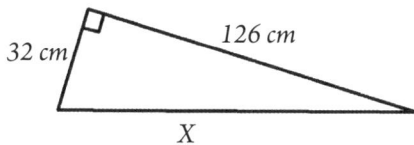

b)

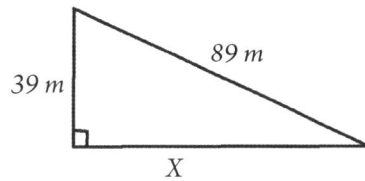

5) Given that *ABCD* is a rectangle, and that:
$$\overline{AB} = 9.6 \text{ m}$$
$$\overline{BC} = 11 \text{ m}$$
$$\overline{AE} = 2.8 \text{ m}$$

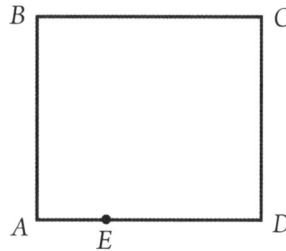

a) What is the area of the rectangle *ABCD*?

b) What is the area of triangle *AEB*?

c) What is the area of triangle *AEC*?

d) What is the area of trapezium *CDEB*?

e) What is the area of the triangle *BCE*?

f) What is the area of the triangle *BDE*?

6) Looking back at the previous worksheet, use the Arabian formula to calculate the values of X, Y and Z for:

a) $u = 5$ and $v = 3$

b) $u = 6$ and $v = 3$

7) The Pythagorean triples that were listed in the Arabian formula table on the previous worksheet were special.

a) What was special about them?

b) Why didn't that table include your answers from the above problem (using $u = 5$, $v = 3$; or $u = 6$, $v = 3$)?

Mental arithmetic

8) $21 \div 999 =$

9) $40 \times 69 =$

10) $700 \times 600 =$

11) $7012 - 5996 =$

12) $45^2 =$

13) $7 \times 99 =$

14) $34 \times 26 =$

15) $900 \div 150 =$

Review

16) At 72 km/h, how far does a car travel in 2 hours and 45 minutes?

17) Pam leaves her house at 11:10, to cycle to Karen's house, which is 39 km away. At what time will she arrive if she averages a rate of 15 km/h?

Geometry – Sheet 6

1) Using the rectangle below:

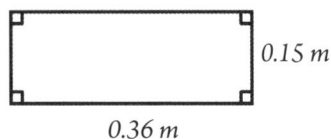

0.15 m

0.36 m

a) What is the perimeter in metres?

b) What is the area in square metres?

c) What is the perimeter in centimetres?

d) What is the area in square centimetres?

2) Given the pentagon below:

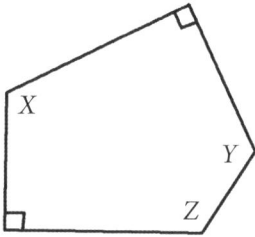

a) What is the sum of the measures of the five angles?

b) If $X = 110°$ and $Y = 118°$, what is Z?

c) If X and Y are congruent, and $Z = 130°$, then what is X?

d) Find X, Y and Z if they are all congruent.

3) *Challenge*
   What are the measures of the three angles in a triangle if the middle-sized angle is 4° more than the smallest angle and 28° less than the largest angle?

4) Find the variables.

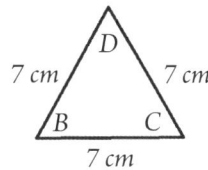

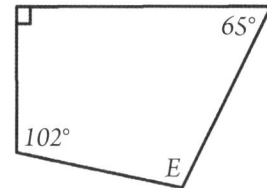

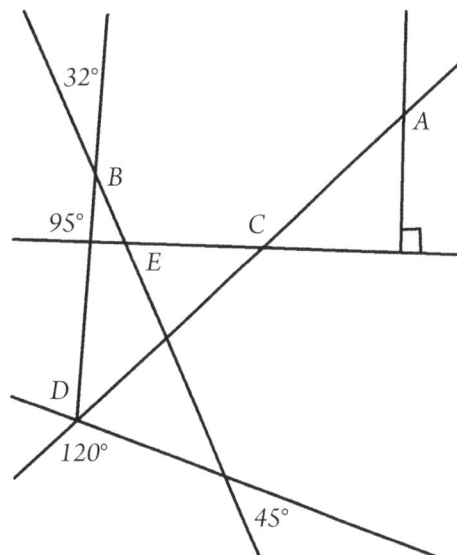

$\angle A =$

$\angle B =$

$\angle C =$

$\angle D =$

$\angle E =$

5) *Challenge*
Find the variables.

Mental arithmetic

6) Multiply:

$$\begin{array}{r} 46 \\ \times 46 \\ \hline \end{array}$$

7) $90 \div 25 =$

8) $95^2 =$

9) $0.39 \div 10{,}000 =$

10) $104^2 =$

11) $13 \times 99 =$

12) $1200 \div 25 =$

13) $12 \times 51 =$

Review

14) Find X given that the two triangles are similar.

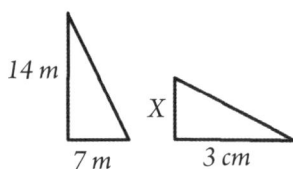

15) $224 \, \text{m}\ell = \underline{\hspace{2cm}} \, \ell$

16) $\frac{3}{4} \, \text{km} = \underline{\hspace{3cm}} \, \text{cm}$

17) *Average speed*
For each problem, don't calculate a value; simply indicate whether the average speed is less than, equal to or greater than 10 km/h.

a) Benny biked from home to the river at 15 km/h and then biked back at 5 km/h.

b) Bob biked 5 km in the first hour, and then 15 km in the second hour.

18) 120 to 216 is what percentage increase?

19) 216 to 120 is what percentage decrease?

20) Jeff bikes at 18 km/h. How far is it from his house to school if it takes him 40 minutes to bike that distance?

21) *Short division*
Leave the answer as a mixed number.
$872{,}345 \div 7$

22) *Division*
Leave the answer as an exact decimal (perhaps repeating).
$72.9 \div 0.074$

Algorithm – Sheet 1

1) State the two laws of repeating decimals.

2) Convert each fraction into an exact decimal:
   a) $\frac{19}{54}$

   b) $\frac{19}{125}$

   c) $\frac{19}{26}$

3) Calculate:
   a) $\sqrt{36}$

   b) $\sqrt{3600}$

   c) $\sqrt{360,000}$

   d) $\sqrt{36,000,000}$

   e) $\sqrt{144}$

   f) $\sqrt{14,400}$

   g) $\sqrt{1,440,000}$

   h) $\sqrt{144,000,000}$

   i) $\sqrt{490,000}$

   j) $\sqrt{900}$

   k) $\sqrt{250,000}$

   l) $\sqrt{40,000}$

   m) $\sqrt{4,000,000}$

4) Look at the previous problems in order to answer the following questions. (Assume that all square roots work out to whole numbers.)
   a) If a number has 3 digits, then its square root will have _____ digits.

   b) If a number has 4 digits, then its square root will have _____ digits.

   c) If a number has 5 digits, then its square root will have _____ digits.

   d) If a number has 6 digits, then its square root will have _____ digits.

   e) If a number has 7 digits, then its square root will have _____ digits.

   f) If a number has 8 digits, then its square root will have _____ digits.

   g) If a number has 25 digits, then its square root will have _____ digits.

   h) If a number has 26 digits, then its square root will have _____ digits.

5) Considering the previous answers, give a general law that states how many digits the answer for any square root problem will have.

Algorithm

109

6) Calculate:

a) 20^2

b) 90^2

c) 400^2

d) 300^2

e) 7000^2

f) 1100^2

g) $80,000^2$

h) 634^2

7) If a number has 3 digits, then squaring it will give a number with _____ digits.

8) Considering the above answer, give a general law that states how many digits the answer for squaring a number will have.

The trial and error method

This method for calculating square roots is quite easy to understand but not very efficient. We simply guess what the answer might be, and then check how good our guess was by squaring it and seeing if it was too big or too small.

Example: Find $\sqrt{2209}$.

We might first guess that the answer is 50, so we check that by squaring 50, which is 2,500, and since 2,500 is greater than 2,209, we know that $\sqrt{2209}$ must be less than 50.

Our next guess may be 42, so we check it by squaring 42, which is 1,764, telling us $\sqrt{2209}$ must be greater than 42. Similarly, we might try 45 (which turns out to be too small) and 48 (which is too big), until we finally narrow the answer down to 47, which is exactly correct since 47^2 is equal to 2,209.

Also, if we know for sure that the square root works out exactly, then the last digit inside the square root can give us a clue to the answer. For example, with 2,209, since the last digit inside the square root is 9, we know that the last digit in our answer must be a 3 or a 7. This is because only 3^2 ($=9$) and 7^2 ($=49$) end with a digit of 9. Again, this only works if we know for sure that the square root works out evenly.

9) Calculate (the answers work out exactly):

a) $\sqrt{1521}$

b) $\sqrt{4624}$

c) $\sqrt{74,529}$

Algorithm – Sheet 2

1) Calculate:

a) $\sqrt{16,000,000}$

b) $\sqrt{90,000}$

c) $\sqrt{1,210,000}$

d) 600^2

e) $15,000^2$

2) For each of the problems below, state the number of digits that the answer will have (before the decimal point), and state what the first digit will be. *Do not calculate the square root exactly.*

Example: $\sqrt{467,856}$
Solution: $\sqrt{467,856}$ has 3 digits and the first digit is 6.
Note: It turns out that $\sqrt{467,856}$ is equal to 684 (which you don't have to calculate).

a) $\sqrt{2601}$ has ____ digits; the first digit is ____.

b) $\sqrt{537,289}$ has ____ digits; the first digit is ____.

c) $\sqrt{1369}$ has ____ digits; the first digit is ____.

d) $\sqrt{79,524}$ has ____ digits; the first digit is ____.

e) $\sqrt{74,390,625}$ has ____ digits; the first digit is ____.

f) $\sqrt{88,209}$ has ____ digits; the first digit is ____.

Using formulas
Galileo's law of falling bodies.
$$D = 4.9 \times T^2$$
This formula tells us something about dropping rocks off cliffs. Specifically, it calculates how many metres the rock will fall *(D)* after being in the air for *T* seconds. (Note: it assumes zero air resistance.)

3) a) How far does a rock fall after being dropped from a cliff for 1 second?

b) How far does a rock fall after being dropped from a cliff for 2 seconds?

c) How far does a rock fall after being dropped from a cliff for 3 seconds?

d) How far does a rock fall after being dropped from a cliff for 5 seconds?

e) How far does a rock fall after being dropped from a cliff for 10 seconds?

f) How high would a cliff need to be in order for a rock to be able to fall for a whole minute before hitting the ground?

Algorithm 111

Heron's formula for the area of a triangle

$$\text{Area} = \sqrt{s(s-a)(s-b)(s-c)}$$

Where s is the semi-perimeter (half the perimeter).

Example: Find the area of the triangle with sides of length 5, 6 and 7 cm.

We set *a, b, c* equal to 5, 6, 7. The perimeter is 18, so *s* is set to 9, which gives us:

$$\text{Area} = \sqrt{9(2)(3)(4)}$$
$$= \sqrt{216}$$
$$\approx 14.7 \text{ cm}^2$$

4) a) Find the area of the triangle with sides of length 6, 8 and 10 metres.

b) Find the area of the triangle with sides of length 13, 14 and 15 metres.

c) Find the area of the triangle with sides of length 3, 5 and 6 cm.

The squaring formula

$$(a+b)^2 = a^2 + b(2a+b)$$

This formula gives us a very different method for calculating the square of a number. It says that if I want to calculate the square of a number (call it *n*), then I can first break it down into two parts, *a* and *b*, such that $a + b = n$, and then put these values for *a* and *b* into the formula in order to get my final answer.

Example: Calculate 17^2 using the squaring formula.

We can choose any two numbers that add to 17, but 10 and 7 are the easiest. Putting these numbers into the formula gives us:

$$17^2 \rightarrow (10+7)^2 = 10^2 + 7(2 \times 10 + 7)$$
$$= 100 + 7(27)$$
$$= 100 + 189$$
$$= 289$$

(which is equal to 17^2)

Note: There are many other possible squaring formulas. This particular one does not save us time for calculating the square of a number. It is, in fact, much easier to get an answer by simply multiplying the number times itself, as we would normally do. The reason that we are using this formula is that it will be of great use for us when we learn a method for calculating square roots – something called the *square root algorithm*.

5) a) Calculate 26^2 by using the squaring formula.

b) Calculate 83^2 by using the squaring formula.

c) Calculate 74^2 by using the squaring formula.

d) Calculate 39^2 by using the squaring formula.

Algorithm – Sheet 3

1) For each of the problems below, state the number of digits that the answer will have (before the decimal point), and the first digit of the answer. Do not calculate what the square root is equal to. (If you need help, then look at the previous worksheet.)

a) $\sqrt{7384}$ has ____ digits; the first digit is ____.

b) $\sqrt{67,482}$ has ____ digits; the first digit is ____.

c) $\sqrt{985,035}$ has ___ digits; the first digit is ____.

d) $\sqrt{803}$ has ____ digits; the first digit is ____.

e) $\sqrt{9,670,564}$ has ___ digits; the first digit is ____.

2) Calculate by using the squaring formula (see previous worksheet).

a) 57^2

b) 14^2

c) 95^2

The long algebraic method
(for two-digit answers)

Example: Calculate $\sqrt{6889}$.
Solution: Here $n = 6,889$. We know that its square root has 2 digits, and that the first digit is 8 (because $\sqrt{68}$ is between 8 and 9). We call our first estimate of the answer a, and in this case $a = 80$. The second digit we call b.

Here is the procedure:
Using the square root identity
$$n - a^2 = b(2a + b)$$
(which comes from $\sqrt{n} = a + b$)
We put in $n = 6889$ and $a = 80$ we get:
$$6889 - 80^2 = b(2 \times 80 + b)$$
$$6889 - 6400 = b(160 + b)$$
$$489 = b(160 + b)$$

Now we determine b (the answer's second digit). We try different single digit values for b to see what works.

For example,
for $b = 2$, then we do 162×2;
for $b = 5$, then we do 165×5,
hoping that one of them will be equal to (or just under) 489. It turns out that $b = 3$ works ($163 \times 3 = 489$). Therefore, our answer is 83. (Since 163×3 is exactly 489, we know that our answer is exact. We can check our answer by squaring 83 to get exactly 6,889.)

Algorithm 113

3) Calculate each square root using the long algebraic method. It is important that you do the problem and organise your work on a separate sheet exactly like the example just given. (Show your workings on a separate paper. All answers work out exactly.)

a) Calculate $\sqrt{3249}$

b) Calculate $\sqrt{5329}$

c) Calculate $\sqrt{784}$

d) Calculate $\sqrt{8464}$

Algorithm – Sheet 4

1) Calculate each square root using the long algebraic method, using the method shown on the previous worksheet (all answers work out exactly):

a) $\sqrt{2025}$

b) $\sqrt{361}$

c) $\sqrt{7056}$

d) $\sqrt{4356}$

The long algebraic method
(*for larger answers*)

For square roots that have answers with more than two digits, we need to do the same procedure as above, but repeat the process a number of times.

Keep in mind that the a values are the digits that we are certain of at a given point, and the b values are the digits that we are trying to figure out.

Notation:

- a_1 means the value of a (with one correct digit) for the first time through the process.
- a_2 means the value of a (with two correct digits) for the second time through the process.

- a_3 means the value of a (with three correct digits) for the third time through the process.
- The values of b are similarly given as b_1, b_2, b_3, etc.

Example: Calculate $\sqrt{7,203,856}$.

- *Step 1*

We know the answer has 4 digits, and the first digit is 2 (because $\sqrt{7}$ is between 2 and 3), so $a_1 = 2,000$, and we use the identity $n - a_1{}^2 = b_1(2a_1 + b_1)$, where $2a_1 = 4,000$.

n 7,203,856
$a_1{}^2$ $- 4,000,000$ (because $2,000^2 = 4,000,000$)
$n - a_1{}^2$ 3,203,856 $= b_1(4000 + b_1)$
                    where b_1 is the 100's place
                    (e.g. 300, 400, etc.)
$b_1 = 600$ because 700 is too big,
which means $b_1(2a_1 + b_1) = 2,760,000$

- *Step 2*

We now know that the first two digits are 2 and 6, so $a_2 = 2600$, and we use the identity $n - a_2{}^2 = b_2(2a^2 + b_2)$, where $2a_2 = 5200$.

n 7,203,856
$a_2{}^2$ $- 6,760,000$ (because $2600^2 = 6,760,000$)
$n - a_2{}^2$ 443,856 $= b_2(5200 + b_2)$
                    where b_2 is the tens' place (e.g. 30, 40)
$b_2 = 80$ because 90 is too big,
which means $b_2(2a_2 + b_2) = 422,400$

- *Step 3*

We now know that the first three digits are 2, 6 and 8,

so $a_3 = 2680$, and we use the identity

$n - a_3^2 = b_3(2a_3 + b_3)$, where $2a_3 = 5{,}360$.

n	7,203,856	
a_3^2	$- 7{,}182{,}400$	(because $2{,}680^2 = 7{,}182{,}400$)
$n - a_3^2$	$21{,}456 = b_3(5360 + b_3)$	

where b_3 is the unit's place (e.g. 3, 4, etc.)

$b_3 = 4$, which means $b_3(2a_3 + b_3) = 21{,}456$

which means that our final answer is *exactly* 2,684.

2) Calculate each square root using the long algebraic method. It is important that you do the problem and organise your work exactly like the example given above. (Show your workings on a separate paper. All answers work out exactly.)

a) $\sqrt{285{,}156}$

b) $\sqrt{71{,}289}$

c) $\sqrt{524{,}176}$

d) $\sqrt{767{,}376}$

Algorithm – Sheet 5

Calculate each square root using the long algebraic method. It is important that you do the problem and organise your work exactly like the example given on the previous worksheet. (Show your workings on a separate paper. All answers work out exactly.)

1) $\sqrt{184{,}041}$

2) $\sqrt{128{,}164}$

3) $\sqrt{34{,}596}$

4) $\sqrt{5{,}593{,}225}$

5) $\sqrt{72{,}131{,}049}$

Algorithm – Sheet 6

1) Calculate each square root using the long algebraic method, as done on the previous worksheets (all answers work out exactly):

a) $\sqrt{403,225}$

b) $\sqrt{61,009}$

c) $\sqrt{24,137,569}$

The short algebraic method

The basic idea is to reduce the amount of calculating. The long algebraic method, described above, requires some tedious, and unnecessary, calculations, which can be eliminated.

Look at example for the long algebraic method shown on Sheet 4. Looking at the left side of each step, we see, for Step 1:

$n - a_1^2$, and then for Step 2: $n - a_2^2$, etc.

Since $a_2 = a_1 + b_1$, we can use the squaring formula $(a + b)^2 = a^2 + b(2a + b)$ to get:

$$a_2^2 = (a_1 + b_1)^2 = a_1^2 + b_1(2a_1 + b_1)$$

This is the key idea: In place of subtracting a_2^2 from n, we can instead subtract the whole of $\{a_1^2 + b_1(2a_1 + b_1)\}$ from n since it is equal to a_2^2. This seems like more work, but it's not – it's less work.

In other words, instead of doing $n - a_2^2$, we can do $n - \{a_1^2 + b_1(2a_1 + b_1)\}$, which is the same as $(n - a_1^2) - \{b_1(2a_1 + b_1)\}$

In short: instead of doing $n - a_2^2$ we do $(n - a_1^2) - \{b_1(2a_1 + b_1)\}$

Likewise, instead of doing $n - a_3^2$ we do $(n - a_2^2) - \{b_2(2a_2 + b_2)\}$

Likewise, instead of doing $n - a_4^2$ we do $(n - a_3^2) - \{b_3(2a_3 + b_3)\}$, etc.

Of course, any sane person would ask, 'Haven't we made things more complicated?' The answer to this is (and this is where the genius of this method comes in):

$(n - a_2^2) - \{b_2(2a_2 + b_2)\}$

is easier to do than

$n - a_3^2$

because a_3^2 requires us to square some big ugly number (e.g. 2,680), whereas we have already calculated both

$(n - a_2^2)$ (443,856 in the example below) and $\{b_2(2a_2 + b_2)\}$ (422,400 below).

Subtracting 443,856 – 422,400, is easier than squaring 2,680!

Example: $\sqrt{7,203,856}$ (once again!):

n	7,203,856		our first estimate (a_1) is 2000.
a_1^2	$-\,4,000,000$		

- *Step 1* $n - a_1^2$ 3,203,856 $= b_1(4000 + b_1)$ → $b_1 = 600$
  $b_1(2a_1 + b_1)$ $-\,2,760,000$

- *Step 2* $n - a_2^2$ 443,856 $= b_2(5200 + b_2)$ → $b_2 = 80$
  $b_2(2a_2 + b_2)$ $-\,422,400$

- *Step 3* $n - a_3^2$ 21,456 $= b_3(5360 + b_3)$ → $b_3 = 4$
  $b_3(2a_3 + ba)$ $-\,21,456$
  0   So our answer is exactly 2684

A Student's Workbook for Mathematics in Class 7

2) Calculate each square root using the short algebraic method. It is important that you do the problem and organise your work exactly like the example given above. Notice that the first three problems are the same ones given in the previous exercise. (All answers work out exactly.)

a) $\sqrt{403{,}225}$

b) $\sqrt{61{,}009}$

c) $\sqrt{24{,}137{,}569}$

d) $\sqrt{393{,}129}$

e) $\sqrt{145{,}924}$

Algorithm – Sheet 7

The square root algorithm
(with zeroes)

This method is basically identical to the short algebraic method, but it cuts out all the unnecessary writing, and there is an added shortcut that aids us in determining the values for $2a_1$, $2a_2$, $2a_3$, etc.

This new shortcut is as follows: With our example of $\sqrt{7{,}203{,}856}$ the values for $2a_1$, $2a_2$, $2a_3$ are 4,000, 5,200, 5,360.

The first of these values is found simply by doubling a_1, which is $2000 \times 2 = 4000$. The rest of these values are found by taking the previous value and adding the new b value to it two times.

So from 4,000, we add b_1 which is 600, giving us 4,600, and then add 600 again, giving us our next value, 5,200.

From 5,200, we add b_2 which is 80, giving us 5,280, and then adding 80 again, gives us our next value, 5,360.

Example: $\sqrt{7{,}203{,}856}$ (once again!)

• *Step 1*
We know that $a_1 = 2{,}000$, so we write down 2,000 twice. Multiplying the two 2,000s gives us the 4,000,000 that is written under 7,203,856, and subtracting, we get 3,203,856.

Then we add 2,000 plus 2,000 to get 4,000, but we put a box in place of the zeroes, and another box underneath the first box. So at this point, everything looks like this:

```
2000              7,203,856
2000            − 4,000,000
4 □              3,203,856
  □
```

It is important to understand that the boxes represent b_1. So at this point, with both the short and long algebraic method, we had had this equation: $3{,}203{,}856 = b_1(4000 + b_1)$, and we asked ourselves, 'what must b_1 be so that $b_1(4000 + b_1)$ is less than 3,203,856?'

Here, with this new method, we are asking essentially the same thing. We need to fill in the two boxes with the same value (i.e. the value for b_1). And this value must be a certain number of hundreds – resulting in a product of 4100×100, or 4200×200, or 4300×300, etc.

Since 4700×700 is bigger than 3,203,856, we put 600 in the two boxes, and write the product of 4600×600, which is 2,760,000, under 3,203,856.

Algorithm

117

• *Step 2*

We now add the left column (4600 + 600), which gives us 5,200, and subtract the right column (3,203,856 − 2,760,000), which is 443,856. Once again, we write a box in place of the zeroes of 5,200, and another box under that one. Everything now looks like this:

```
2000        7,203,856
2000      − 4,000,000
4600        3,203,856
 600      − 2,760,000
52□          443,856
 □
```

Similarly to Step 1, we need to put the same number (which is the tens' place of our final answer) into both boxes so that the resulting product is less than 443,856.

The possibilities are 5210 × 10, or 5220 × 20, or 5230 × 30, etc. Since 5290 × 90 is a bit too big, we put 80 into both boxes, and write the product of 5280 × 80, which is 422,400, under 443,856.

• *Step 3*

We add the left column and subtract the right column, resulting in 5,360 and 21,456, respectively.

We put a box in place of the zero in 5,360, and a box below it (which is not shown below). We can put 4 into both boxes, resulting in 5364 × 4, which is exactly 21,456.

The end result, is that all of our work looks like this (quite short, actually!):

```
2000        7,203,856
2000      − 4,000,000
4600        3,203,856
 600      − 2,760,000
5280          443,856
  80        − 422,400
5364           21,456
   4         − 21,456
                    0
```

The answer, 2,684, comes from the underlined digits.

A remainder of zero tells us that our answer is exact.

This method of the square root algorithm is slightly different from what is done in Class 8.

1) Do each problem three times. First using the long algebraic method; secondly, using the short algebraic method and lastly, using the square root algorithm as described in the example above. (Show your calculations on a separate sheet.)

a) $\sqrt{725{,}904}$

b) $\sqrt{72{,}361}$

c) $\sqrt{28{,}761{,}769}$

2) Do each problem using the square root algorithm only.

a) $\sqrt{665{,}856}$

b) $\sqrt{6{,}041{,}764}$

Algorithm – Sheet 8

Calculate each square root using only the square root algorithm, as shown on the previous sheet:

1) $\sqrt{2116}$

2) $\sqrt{327,184}$

3) $\sqrt{413,449}$

4) $\sqrt{683,929}$

5) $\sqrt{18,395,521}$

6) $\sqrt{86,620,249}$

Algorithm

119

Algebra – Sheet 1

Formulas

1) At Bob Rent-a-Car, the rates are £28 per day and £0.08/mile.

a) What is the formula that is used to calculate the cost (C)?
(*Hint: D* for the number of days and *M* for the number of miles.)

Use the above formula to calculate the cost for renting a car at Bob Rent-a-Car for:

b) 10 days and 900 miles.

c) 7 days and 345 miles.

2) Galileo's law of falling bodies is given by the formula:
$D = 4.9 \times T^2$
where D is the number of metres an object falls (ignoring air resistance) after being dropped for T seconds. Find the distance that an object falls after being dropped for:

a) 3 seconds.

b) 5½ seconds

Signed numbers

Simplify by combining the signed numbers.

3) $6 - 2 - 17$

4) $-5 + 12$

5) $12 - 5$

6) $4 - 6$

7) $-6 + 4$

8) $-10 - 3 - 6$

9) $10 + 3 + 6$

10) $-10 - 3 - 6 + 10 + 3 + 6$

11) $-3 + 8 - 12 - 5 + 4$

12) $8 + 4 - 3 - 12 - 5$

13) $9 - 2 - 6 + 15 - 11$

14) $-2 - 6 - 11 + 9 + 15$

Expressions

Simplify by combining like terms:

15) $3x + 7x$

16) $4x + 9x$

17) $20x - 5x$

18) $3x + 6x + 4x$

19) $2x + 8x + 6x + 13x$

20) $2x + 8y + 6x + 13y$

Equations

Solve each equation, by finding the value for x that makes the equation balance.

21) $x = 21 + 8$

22) $x + 7 = 10$

23) $x = 13 - 8$

24) $x - 4 = 20$

25) $x = 14 \times 3$

26) $x \times 5 = 35$

27) $5x = 35$

28) $x = 42 \div 7$

29) $x \div 3 = 12$

Algebra – Sheet 2

Formulas

1) At Bob Rent-a-Car (see previous sheet), what is the cost of renting a car for 20 days and 700 miles?

2) Find the distance that an object falls after being dropped for 4 seconds (see previous sheet for Galileo's formula).

3) *Gauss's formula* for summing together a sequence of numbers is:
$S = \frac{n}{2} \times (F + L)$
where F is the first number
L is the last number, and
n is the number of numbers.
Find the sum of each sequence of numbers:

a) $40 + 41 + \ldots + 50$

b) $300 + 301 + \ldots + 700$

Signed numbers

Simplify by combining the signed numbers.

4) $5 - 8$

5) $-8 + 5$

6) $13 - 9$

7) $-9 + 13$

8) $-3 + 8 - 2 - 7 + 9$

9) $7 - 18 + 10 - 13 + 4$

10) $-7 - 5 - 9$

11) $-9 + 100$

12) $46 - 70$

13) $-46 - 70$

14) $\frac{3}{8} - \frac{7}{8}$

15) $-\frac{3}{8} + \frac{4}{5}$

16) $-\frac{5}{9} - \frac{4}{7}$

Expressions

Simplify by combining like terms:

17) $5x + 9x$

18) $9x + 5x$

19) $6x - 4x$

20) $-4x + 6x$

21) $3x + 5x + 6x$

22) $6x + x$

23) $3x - 5x$

24) $8x + 4y + 6y - 3x$

25) $8x + 4 + 6 - 3x$

Equations

Solve each equation, by finding the value for x that makes the equation balance:

26) $x = 5 \times 3$

27) $6x = 24$

28) $x + 12 = 15$

29) $x + 12 = 7$

30) $x - 10 = 4$

31) $x - 10 = -4$

32) $x - 10 = -14$

Algebra – Sheet 3

Formulas

1) Find the sum of:
   $213 + 214 + \ldots + 262$.

2) The temperature conversion formulas are:
$$C = \frac{5}{9} \times (F - 32)$$
$$F = \frac{9}{5} \times C + 32$$

Use these formulas to:
a) Convert 25°C to Fahrenheit.

b) Convert 30°C to Fahrenheit.

c) Convert 86°F to Celsius.

d) Convert 50°F to Celsius.

Signed numbers
Simplify:

3) $-7 + 9$

4) $11 - 19$

5) $-19 + 11$

6) $9 - 20 - 4 + 33 - 7$

7) $-9 - 15 - 2$

8) $\frac{2}{5} - \frac{2}{3}$

9) $-\frac{3}{13} - \frac{5}{13}$

10) $(5)(9)$

11) $(-5)(-9)$

12) $(-5)(9)$

13) $(5)(-9)$

14) $(-2)(15)$

15) $(-6)(-7)$

16) $(3)(-10)$

17) $(-120)(-110)$

Expressions
Simplify by combining like terms:

18) $6x + 21x$

19) $2x - 7x$

20) $-7x + 2x$

21) $-4x - 6x$

22) $3x + 5y + 6x$

23) $x + x$

24) $4y + 8x - y - 13x$

25) $-9x - 4 - 12 - 3x$

Equations
Solve each equation. Always check that your answer is correct.

26) $x + 1 = 7$

27) $x - 1 = 7$

28) $5x = 45$

29) $x \div 4 = 20$

30) $x - 10 = -6$

31) $x + 5 = -3$

32) $x \div 3 = 12$

33) $2x = 11$

34) Use guess and check!
$2x + 5 = 19$

Algebra – Sheet 4

Formulas

1) Convert 104°F to Celsius.

2) Convert 5°C to Fahrenheit.

3) Convert 5°F to Celsius.

4) Convert 12°C to Fahrenheit.

5) Convert –13°F to Celsius.

6) Convert –20°C to Fahrenheit.

7) Convert –40°F to Celsius.

Signed numbers

Simplify:

8) $-9 + 13$

9) $-9 - 13$

10) $23 - 32$

11) $-32 + 23$

12) $(3)(6)$

13) $(3)(-6)$

14) $3 - 6$

15) $(-3)(+6)$

16) $-3 + 6$

17) $(-3)(-6)$

18) $-3 - 6$

19) $(-15) \div (-3)$

20) $(15) \div (-3)$

21) $\dfrac{15}{-3}$

22) $7 - (-4)$

23) $5 - (+9)$

24) $-4 - (-6)$

25) $-7 - (-3 - 5)$

Expressions

Simplify by combining like terms:

26) $5x + 7x$

27) $3a + 6b - 8a$

28) $9 + 5x - 4$

29) $y + 4 + x - 12 - 5x + y$

30) $3x - 73 + 10x$

31) $5x + 13 - 5x - 2$

32) $5x - 8y - x + 6$

33) $-7 + x - 8 - 4x$

One-step equations

Solve each equation by getting x alone.
Show what is done to each side. Check your
answers with the previous sheet.

Example: $x + 7 = 10$
$$\underline{-7 \quad -7}$$
$$x \quad = \quad 3$$

34) $x + 1 = 7$

35) $x - 1 = 7$

36) $5x = 45$

37) $x \div 4 = 20$

38) $x - 10 = -6$

39) $x + 5 = -3$

40) $x \div 3 = 12$

41) $2x = 11$

Algebra – Sheet 5

Formulas

See previous sheets (pp. 120, 122) for formulas.

1) At Bob Rent-a-Car, what is the cost of renting a car for 15 days and 1000 miles?

2) Find the distance that an object falls after being dropped for 1½ seconds.

3) Convert 20°C to Fahrenheit.

4) Convert 20°F to Celsius (to the nearest ½°).

5) Find the sum of $8 + 9 + 10 + \ldots + 67$.

Signed numbers
Simplify:

6) $-2 + 9$

7) $-5 + 1$

8) $-5 - 1$

9) $19 - 33$

10) $(5)(-7)$

11) $5 - 7$

12) $(-3)(8)$

13) $-3 + 8$

14) $(-4)(-3)$

15) $-4 - 3$

16) $(14) \div (-2)$

17) $(-14) \div (2)$

18) $\frac{-14}{2}$

19) $(-14) \div (-2)$

20) $\frac{-14}{-2}$

21) $10 - (-8)$

22) $9 - (+2)$

23) $9 + (-2)$

24) $-12 - (-5)$

25) $-7 - (-3) + -5 - (+4)$

Expressions
Simplify by combining like terms:

26) $x + x + x + a + a$

27) $7a - 5y + 8 - a + 12y$

28) $4 + x - 5b - 5x + 7 + x$

29) $x - 6y + 5 - x - 5 + 8y$

30) $8x - 7 - 13x - 8$

31) $-3x - 2 - x + 9$

32) $-x + 5 + 6x - 8$

One-step equations
Solve each equation by getting x alone.
Show what is done to each side. Check that
your answers are correct.

33) $x + 5 = 8$

34) $x + 12 = 8$

35) $x - 7 = 10$

36) $x - 8 = -2$

37) $3x = 21$

38) $x \div 10 = 7$

39) $x + 9 = -4$

40) $x \div 5 = 9$

41) $2x = 8$

42) $\frac{1}{2}x = 8$

Algebra – Sheet 6

Formulas

A perfect number is one that is equal to the sum of its divisors, for instance, 6 (divisors 1, 2 and 3; $1 + 2 + 3 = 6$).

Euclid's formula for perfect numbers is:

$$p = (2^{(n-1)}) \times (2^n - 1),$$

where p is a perfect number only if $(2^n - 1)$ is a prime number.

1) Calculate the first three perfect numbers after 6, by using the above formula, and putting in $n = 2$, and then $n = 3$, and then $n = 4$, etc. Don't forget to check that $(2^n - 1)$ is prime. (Show your work on a separate sheet.)

Signed numbers

Simplify:

2) $-5 - 10$

3) $-4 + 12$

4) $-9 + 4$

5) $6 - 14$

6) $(-5)(-8)$

7) $(-5)(3)$

8) $(-18) \div (-6)$

9) $\frac{-18}{-6}$

10) $(18) \div (-6)$

11) $\frac{35}{-5}$

12) $-4 - (-10)$

13) $-5 - (+8)$

14) $-12 + 25 - 6 - 3$

15) $5 - (-6) + (-8) - (+7)$

Expressions

Simplify by combining like terms:

16) $7x - 8 + 2x$

17) $7x - 8 + 2$

18) $7 - 3x + 5 - 6x$

19) $x - 5 + 5x + 2$

20) $7 - x - 3 + 6x - 1$

21) $-7x + 9 + 5x - 2x$

22) $y - 7 + 8 - 4a - 3y + x$

Solving equations

Solve each equation by getting x alone. Show what is done to each side. Check that your answers are correct.

23) $5x = 40$

24) $5x = -40$

25) $-5x = -40$

26) $-5 + x = 40$

27) $5x + 1 = 3x + 9$

28) $7x + 5 = 4x + 26$

29) $5x - 7 = x + 3$

30) $8x + 19 = 3$

31) $-7x + 4 = -31$

32) $x - 7 + 6x = 8 - x + 9$

Algebra – Sheet 7

Signed numbers

Simplify:

1) $-8 + 13$

2) $20 - 50$

3) $(5)(-9)$

4) $(-4)(-6)$

5) $(-28) \div (-4)$

6) $(16) \div (-2)$

7) $\frac{16}{-2}$

8) $-5 \times \frac{-3}{5}$

9) $\frac{3}{4} \times \frac{-16}{27}$

10) $5 - (-9)$

11) $-8 - 2 + 6 - 7 + 4$

12) $-5 + -9 - (+7) - (-2)$

Expressions

Simplify by combining like terms:

13) $7x + 6 - 12x$

14) $-6 - 7x - 8$

15) $-4x - 5 - x + 10$

16) $8b + 4a - b - 4$

Solving equations

Solve each equation by getting x alone. Show what is done to each side. Check that your answers are correct.

17) $4x = 28$

18) $3x = -21$

19) $x + 6 = 2$

20) $x - 4 = 11$

21) $-4x = 12$

22) $x \div 3 = 15$

23) $\frac{x}{3} = 15$

24) $-8x = -4$

25) $5x - 4 = 2x + 23$

26) $2x + 11 = 9x - 3$

27) $6x - 5 + 2x = 17 + 15x - 77$

28) $4x - 5 - x - 3 = -2x + 4 + 9x$

29) *Challenge*
$-18x - 5 + x + 4 + 38x - x - 5 = 3x - 18 - 5x + 30 + 9x - 5$

Algebra – Sheet 8

Signed numbers
Simplify:

1) $-8 - 3$

2) $34 - 42$

3) $(4)(-7)$

4) $(-8)(-3)$

5) $(40) \div (-4)$

6) $(-20) \div (-5)$

7) $\frac{-20}{-5}$

8) $6 \times \frac{7}{-15}$

9) $\left(\frac{-4}{5}\right) \times \left(\frac{-5}{6}\right)$

10) $-7 - (-10)$

11) $-6 + 9 + 4 - 7$

12) $-2 - (-7) + (-8)$

Solving equations
Solve each equation by getting x alone.
Show what is done to each side. Check that
your answers are correct.

13) $-5x = -40$

14) $x + 7 = -2$

15) $6x = -42$

16) $x \div 4 = 8$

17) $\frac{x}{4} = 8$

18) $7x - 21 = 3x - 9$

19) $8x + 3 - 5x = 7 - 4x - 32$

20) $x - 8 - 6x = -7 + x - 3$

21) $6x - 7 = 2x - 10$

22) *Challenge*

$\frac{1}{6}x + \frac{2}{3} - \frac{3}{4}x = -\frac{7}{10} + \frac{2}{3}x - \frac{2}{5}$

23) *Challenge*

$7x+4-x-8-11x-14 = -12+49x+23-11-52x$

24) *Challenge*

$-x-2\frac{2}{3}-12x+13+5x-5\frac{1}{2} = 13\frac{2}{3}x+5-\frac{3}{4}x-21\frac{1}{6}-17\frac{5}{12}x$

Class Six Maths Tricks

Multiplication and zeroes. When multiplying two numbers, ignore all ending zeroes, do the multiplication and then add the zeroes back onto the answer.

Example: For 4000 × 300,
we multiply 4 times 3,
and then add on the 5 zeroes
giving a result of 1,200,000.

Division and zeroes. When dividing two numbers that both end in zeroes, cancel the same number of ending zeroes from each of the two numbers, then do the division problem.

Example: For 24,000 ÷ 600,
we cancel two zeroes from both numbers,
and then divide 240 by 6 to get 40.

Multiplying and dividing by 10, 100, 1000, etc. Simply move the decimal point!

Example: 634.6 ÷ 100 = 6.346
We move the decimal point 2 places because there are 2 zeroes in 100.

Example: 48.37 × 1000 = 48,370
The decimal point gets moved 3 places since there are 3 zeroes in 1,000.

Adding numbers by grouping. Search for digits that add up to 10 or 20.

Example: For 97 + 86 + 13 + 42 + 54,
we see that with the units' digits we can add 7 + 3 and 6 + 4 to make ten twice,
leaving the 2 (from the 42) left over.
The sum of the units' column is therefore 22.
In the tens' column, the carry of 2 combines with the 8 to form 10, as does the 9 and the 1.
We are left with the 4 and 5.
The tens' column is therefore 29.
Our answer is 292.

Multiplying by 4. You can instead double the number two times.

Example: For 4 × 35,
we double 35 to get 70,
and double again to get a result of 140.

Multiplying a 2-digit number by 11. Separate the digits, and then insert the sum of the digits in-between.

Example: For 62 × 11,
6 plus 2 is 8,
so we place the 8 between the 6 and the 2,
giving a result of 682.

Example: For 75 × 11,
7 plus 5 is 12,
so we place the 2 between the 7 and 5
and carry the 1, giving 825.

Multiplying two numbers that are just over 100. First write down a 1, then next to the one we write down the sum of how far above 100 the two numbers are and then the product of how far above 100 the two numbers are. Both the sum and the product must be two digits.

Example: For 105 × 102,
add 5 plus 2 (to get 07),
and then multiply 5 times 2 (to get 10),
giving 10,710.

Example: For 112 × 107,
we do 12 + 7 (19)
and then 12 × 7 (84),
which leads to an answer of 11,984.

Dividing by 4. You can instead cut the number in half, two times.

Example: For 64 ÷ 4,
we take half of 64 to get 32,
and then take half of that
for a result of 16.

Subtraction by adding distances. Pick an 'easy' number between the two numbers, and add the distances from each of the numbers to the easy number.

Example: For 532 − 497,
  choose 500 as the easy number.
  The distance from 532 to 500 is 32
  and the distance from 497 to 500 is 3.
  The answer is therefore 32+3, which is 35.

Division by nines. When dividing two numbers where the divisor's digits are all nines, we get a decimal where the dividend repeats, but the number of repeating digits must be equal to the number of nines.

Example: $38 \div 99 = 0.\overline{38}$
Example: $417 \div 999 = 0.\overline{417}$
Example: $62 \div 999 = 0.\overline{062}$

Multiplying by nines.

Method 1: Multiply by 10, 100 or 1000, and then subtract the original number.

Example: For 47×99,
  we do $100 \times 47 - 47$,
  which is 4,700−47,
  giving an answer of 4,653.

Method 2 (for single digits): Multiply the single digit by 9, which gives us a two-digit answer. Then separate these two digits and insert one less nine than what was in the original problem.

Example: For 8×9999,
  we multiply 8 times 9,
  which gives us 72.
  Then we insert three nines
  between the 7 and the 2,
  giving a final answer of 79,992.

Reducing before dividing. Any division problem is viewed as a fraction that can often be reduced.

Example: For 3500÷2800,
  we reduce the fraction to ⁵⁄₄,
  which is 1¼ or 1.25.

Multiplying by 5. Take half the number, and then add a zero, or move the decimal point.

Example: For 5×26,
  we take half of 26 to get 13,
  and then add a zero,
  giving us a result of 130.

Example: For 5×4.18,
  half of 4.18 is 2.09,
  and moving the decimal point
  to the right one place gives 20.9.

Dividing by 5. Double the number, and then divide by ten (move the decimal one place to the left).

Example: For $80 \div 5$,
  we double 80
  and then chop off a zero,
  giving a result of 16.

Example: For $93 \div 5$,
  we double 93
  and then move the decimal point
  one place to the left to get 18.6.

Class Seven Maths Tricks

Multiplying two numbers that are just one above and below a number that is easy to square. The answer is one less than the square of the 'easy' number between them.

Example: For 29×31,
    we square 30,
    and then subtract 1,
    giving a result of 899.

Multiplying by 25. You can instead take half the number, two times, and then add two zeroes.

Example: For 25×48,
    take half of 48 to get 24,
    and half again to get 12.
    Adding two zeroes gives 1200.

Squaring a number ending in 5. Multiply the tens' digit by the next whole number, then place 25 at the end.

Example: For 65^2,
    you multiply 6 times 7,
    which is 42,
    and then add 25 at the end
    to get 4225 as a result.

Dividing by 25. Instead, double the number two times, then divide by 100 (move decimal left two places).

Example: For $108 \div 25$,
    we double 108 to get 216,
    and then double it again to get 432.
    Our answer is 4.32.

Multiplying a number by 15 (or 15%). Multiply the number by ten, then add that product to half of itself.

Example: For 32×15,
    we add 320 with 160
    (which is ½ of 320),
    giving a result of 480.

Example: For 15% of 420,
    we add 10% of 420 (which is 42)
    to half of that (which is 21),
    resulting in 63.

Multiplying an even number by a number ending in 5. Cut the even number in half, and double the number ending in 5. Multiply the results.

Example: For 14×45,
    half of 14 is 7,
    and twice 45 is 90,
    giving a result of 7 times 90,
    which is 630.

Dividing by a number ending in 5. Double both numbers, then divide.

Example: For $180 \div 45$,
    we double both numbers,
    giving $360 \div 90$,
    which is 4.

Multiplying two numbers that have the same tens' digits and have units' digits that add to 10. Multiply the tens' digit by the next whole number, and then place the product of the units' digits at the end, as two digits.

Example: For 47×43,
    we do 4 times 5 ($= 20$),
    and then 7 times 3 ($= 21$),
    giving a result of 2,021.

Squaring a two-digit number beginning in 5. Add 25 to the units' digit, then place the square of the units' digit (as two digits) at the end.

Example: For 53^2,
    we add $25 + 3$ (which is 28),
    then we square 3 (which is 09),
    giving a result of 2,809.

Multiplying two numbers that are an equal distance from a number that is easy to square. Subtract the square of the distance from the square of the easy number.

Example: For 34×26,
    we notice that the numbers
    are both 4 from 30.
    The result is $30^2 - 4^2 = 884$.

Squaring a two-digit number ending in 1. Write down a 1. Add the tens' digit to itself, and write down the units' digit of that answer to the left of the 1 that was first written down and carry a 1 if it was greater than ten. Now multiply the tens' digit by itself, and add 1 if you had a carry and write down the result to the left of all that was previously written down. It's easier than you think!

Example: For 71^2,
    we write down a 1,
    add 7 plus 7,
    write down the 4
    (to the left of the original 1),
    and carry the 1.
    Lastly we multiply 7 times 7,
    and add the 1 that was carried.
    The answer is 5,041.

Multiplying by an 'almost easy' number. Do the multiplication with the easy number, and then adjust.

Example: For 12×39,
    we see that 39 is almost 40,
    so we multiply 12 times 40 (which is 480),
    and then we adjust by subtracting 12
    (because 480 is one 12 too much),
    giving 468 as our result.

Example: For 25×31,
    we see that 31 is almost 30,
    so we multiply 25 times 30 (which is 750),
    and then add another 25,
    giving us a result of 775.

Multiplying two 2-digit numbers. Multiply the 2 units digits to get the answer's units' digit. Carry, if necessary. Cross-multiply to get the tens' digit (see example below). Carry, if necessary. Multiply the 2 numbers' tens' digits in order to get the hundreds' place in the answer.

Example (without carrying): For 12×23,
    the answer has a units' digit of 2 times 3 = **6**.
    Now we cross-multiply
    to get the answer's tens' digit,
    which is 2 times 2, plus 1 times 3,
    which is **7**.
    The answer's hundreds' place
    is just 1 times 2, which is **2**.
    Our final answer (see underlined digits)
    is then 276.

Example (with carrying): For 47×28,
    we first multiply 7 times 8 (which is 56),
    which means the answer's units' digit is **6**
    with a carry of 5.
    Then, we cross multiply for the tens' digit
    (see work below), doing 7 times 2,
    plus 4 times 8, plus 5 (the carry),
    to get 51.
    This means the answer's tens' place is **1**,
    with a carry of 5.
    Finally, we multiply 4 times 2
    and add 5 (the carry),
    which gives **13**.
    The final answer (see underlined digits above)
    is 1,316.

$$
\begin{array}{r}
4\ \ 7 \\
\times\ 2\ \ 8 \\
\hline
1\ 3\ 1\ 6
\end{array}
$$

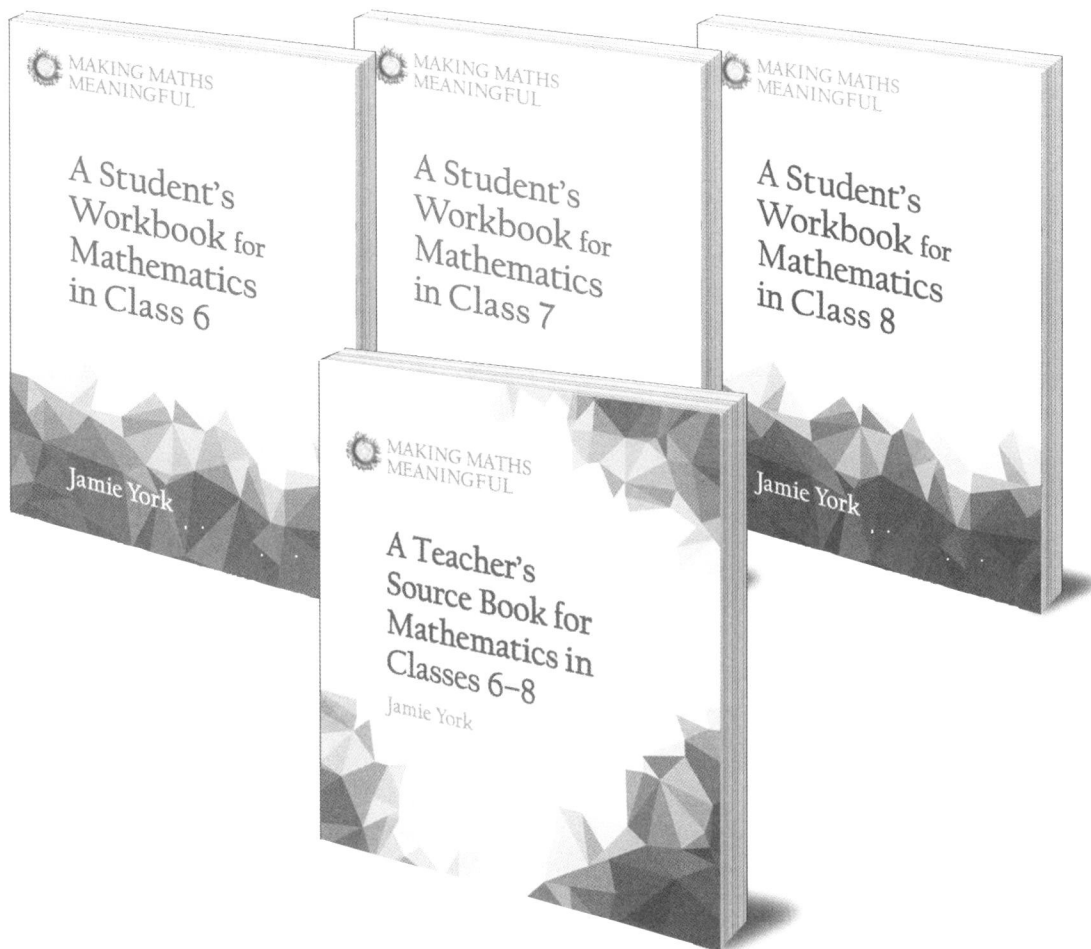

First published in the United States of America
by Jamie York Press, Boulder CO in 2009
www.JamieYorkPress.com
First published in the UK in 2016
by Floris Books, Edinburgh,
adapted from the 2015 American edition

British Library CIP Data available
ISBN 978-178250-320-0
Printed in Great Britain
by Bell & Bain Ltd